Breakfasts & Brunches

D1536008

CYNTHIA SCHEER
Writer and Food Stylist

JILL FOX
Project Editor

LINDA HINRICHS
CAROL KRAMER
Designers

DENNIS GRAY
Photographer

SARA SLAVIN
Photographic Stylist

Danielle Walker *(far left)* is chairman of the board and founder of the California Culinary Academy. **Cynthia Scheer** *(left)* is a food writer and home economist. She has been a magazine food editor and is the author of 15 cookbooks on a variety of subjects. Other books by Cynthia Scheer in the California Culinary Academy series include *Affordable Elegant Meals, Breads, Salads,* and *Soups & Stews.* A resident of the San Francisco Bay Area, she has traveled extensively throughout the United States, Mexico, and Europe to explore and experience the foods of many regions.

The California Culinary Academy Among the forefront of American institutions leading the culinary renaissance in this country, the California Culinary Academy in San Francisco has gained a reputation as one of the most outstanding professional chef training schools in the world. With a teaching staff recruited from the best restaurants of Western Europe, the California Culinary Academy educates students from around the world in the preparation of classical cuisine. The recipes in this book were created in consultation with the chefs of the California Culinary Academy. For information about the Academy, write the Office of the Dean, California Culinary Academy, 625 Polk St., San Francisco, CA 94102.

Front Cover

This colorful brunch menu features Scrambled Eggs in a Crisp Crust (page 50), accompanied by Four Seasons Fresh Fruit Bowl (page 30), and Italian Jam-Filled Crescents (page 124).

Title Page

A breakfast in bed, like this one featuring a Shrimp and Avocado Omelet (page 52), makes a perfect lazy-morning meal.

Back Cover

Upper left: A rich veal stock of leeks, carrots, potatoes, onions, garlic, and herbs can be used in a variety of ways for everything from soup to sauces.

Upper right: Pink Fruit Juice Froth is a blend of strawberries, watermelon, oranges, and limes whirled together for an eye-opening juice that's as pretty to look at as it is delicious. Morning beverages—coffees, teas, juices, and specialty drinks—are featured beginning on page 12.

Lower left: Tiny peeled shrimp are hidden within the springtime brunch classic Asparagus and Seafood Quiche. A chapter devoted to Breakfast Pies begins on page 98.

Lower right: Rosettes of whipped cream, piped onto a chocolate cake with a pastry bag and an open-star tip, are a finishing touch that adds a professional look.

Contributors

Calligrapher
Chuck Wertman

Illustrator
Ellen Blonder

Consultant
Maggie Blyth Klein

Additional Photographers
Michael Lamotte, front cover, back cover: upper left and lower right
Laurie Black, Academy photography
Fischella, photograph of Danielle Walker

Additional Food Stylists
Amy Nathan, front cover, back cover: upper left and lower right
Jeff Van Hanswyk, at the Academy

Photographic Assistant
Mindy Goldfein

Editorial Staff
Mary Lou Carlson
Kathy Kaiser
Rebecca Pepper

Art and Production Staff
Linda Bouchard
Deborah Cowder
Lezlly Freier
Anne Pederson

Lithographed in U.S.A. by
Webcrafters, Inc.

Special Thanks
Beans & Leaves Coffee and Tea, San Francisco and Belmont, CA;
BIA Cordon Bleu, Belmont, CA;
Mr. and Mrs. Steve Cooper;
Fran Flanagan; Mr. and Mrs. Robert Johnson; Anne Kupper, Williams-Sonoma, San Francisco, CA;
Anne McKay; Karen Usas

The California Culinary Academy series is produced by the staff of Ortho Information Services.

Publisher
Robert L. Iacopi

Production Director
Ernie S. Tasaki

Series Managing Editor
Sally W. Smith

Address all inquiries to:
Ortho Information Services
Chevron Chemical Company
Consumer Products Division
575 Market Street
San Francisco, CA 94105
Copyright © 1985
Chevron Chemical Company
All rights reserved under international and Pan-American copyright conventions.

1 2 3 4 5 6 7 8 9

85 86 87 88 89 90

ISBN 0-89721-049-2
Library of Congress Catalog Card Number 85-072803

Chevron Chemical Company
575 Market Street, San Francisco, CA 94105

C O N T E N T S

Breakfasts & Brunches

NUTRITION — 4

Breakfast Foods — 6
Choosing a Nutritious
  Breakfast — 7
What Makes a Good
  Frying Pan — 8

BEVERAGES — 12

Coffee — 14
Special Pots for Special
  Coffees — 15
Breakfast Tea — 18
Hot Chocolate — 18
Fruit Juices — 21
Breakfast in a Glass — 19
Champagne and Other
  Brunch Drinks — 22

FRUITS — 26

Seasonal Fruit — 28
Fall Family Breakfast — 37

EGGS — 38

Eggs Cooked in the Shell — 41
Fried Eggs — 42
Poached Eggs — 44
Eggs Benedict Brunch
  for Eight — 47
Scrambled Eggs — 49
Omelets & Frittatas — 51
Baked Eggs — 55
Soufflés — 57

MEATS, POULTRY & FISH — 62

Beef, Pork & Lamb — 64
Breakfast Potatoes — 66
Make Your Own Pork
  Sausage — 67
Poultry — 69
Tailgate Brunch — 72
Fish & Shellfish — 74

PANCAKES & WAFFLES — 80

Pancakes — 82
Crêpes — 84
Special Pans for Special
  Pancakes — 85
Oven Pancakes — 94
French Toast — 95
Waffles — 96
Breakfast in Bed — 97

BREAKFAST PIES — 98

Quiches — 100
Savory Filo-Wrapped
  Pastries — 104
Filled Loaves & Pastries — 105
Patio Brunch — 106
Fruit Tarts — 109

BREADS & CAKES — 110

Quick Breads — 112
Yeast Breads — 118
Croissants — 121
Swiss Christmas Breakfast — 123

Index — 126
Metric Chart — 128

This breakfast on a tray is a light yet healthy meal that everyone can enjoy. Include a nutritious helping from every food group every day.

nutrition

It may be that the world is divided into two groups: those who can hardly wait for the first nourishment of the day and those who can't face food until a little later. Either way, this book has something for you: breakfast for the eager or brunch for the slow-to-come-around. Breakfast gives a fine foundation for morning's jobs— nutritionists claim that a healthy breakfast keeps you moving efficiently for hours. Brunch, a late-morning meal combining the best elements of breakfast and lunch, is less sensible but more fun.

Brighten up the daily news with sliced fruit on your ready-to-eat cereal. Served with juice, milk, and coffee, cold cereal provides a quick, nutritious meal.

BREAKFAST FOODS

What you eat in the morning may depend on how much time you have and on the eating patterns with which you grew up. Unfortunately, breakfast is often the most rushed meal of the day. That limits some people to a cup of coffee on the run, which is scarcely any breakfast at all. In only a few minutes, you can augment that with a glass of juice, toast or a muffin, and a bowl of ready-to-eat cereal with milk—making a better-balanced repast.

In other parts of the world, breakfast may be the classic Continental combination of coffee and steaming milk, accompanied by freshly baked bread or rolls, lots of butter, and a dollop of fruit preserves or honey.

In Germany or Holland, this is often expanded (and made somewhat more satisfying) by adding a wedge of cheese, a soft-cooked egg, or even a slice of sausage. In Scandinavia, wonderful rye and whole grain breads appear at breakfast, a meal that sometimes becomes a veritable smorgasbord with the addition of cheeses and herring or other fish. The English appear to take the prize for ambitious breakfasts, with hot porridge followed by bacon, sausage, or even kippered herring and grilled tomatoes with eggs.

So it's clear that the foods you choose for breakfast need not become routine. Plenty of variety is available to tempt and nourish you.

CHOOSING A NUTRITIOUS BREAKFAST

You hear a lot about eating a "good" breakfast, but it's useful to clarify how food experts define goodness.

In terms of *quantity*, breakfast should account for a fourth to a third of the day's food energy or calories. After all, your body needs fuel to run on during the morning. Consider the meaning of the word *breakfast*—to break the fast of the night before.

Even if you are counting calories, you are entitled to at least a fourth of the day's allotment at breakfast. It seems that by beginning the day with a satisfying meal, you are less likely to overeat at lunch, dinner, or in between.

The *quality* of breakfast depends on the food you choose. Black coffee and a sugary doughnut, for example, contain little but carbohydrates, fat, and possibly a few B vitamins. Your body deserves more than that.

A simple guide for selecting healthy breakfasts—and other meals, as well—is the division of all foods into the Basic Four Food Plan. The four food groups are: (1) milk and other dairy products, (2) meat and other protein foods (fish, poultry, eggs, cheese, dried peas and beans, and nuts), (3) fruits and vegetables, and (4) breads and cereals.

Use the Basic Four Food Plan to make breakfast choices that are good for you: fruits and vegetables, meats and proteins, dairy products, and breads and cereals. The recipe for Orange-Date Muffins is on page 114.

Nutritionists suggest that for breakfast you include foods from at least three of these four groups. The morning meal is a good time to get the vitamin C (ascorbic acid) you need every day. Good sources include citrus fruits and juices (orange or grapefruit), strawberries, cantaloupe, and tomato juice.

If all this sounds too predictable to you, you are probably the sort of person who would enjoy practically any kind of food for breakfast. And why not? A good breakfast can take many forms.

Leaf through this book and you will find a variety of options: nutritious fruit shakes that make a quick, delicious breakfast-in-a-glass; fresh strawberry shortcake with whipped cream and buttery homemade biscuits; speedy breakfast pizza on broiled English muffins; grilled cheese-and-tomato sandwiches. Each of these includes a nutritionally significant amount of food from each of the four basic groups.

WHAT MAKES A GOOD FRYING PAN?

If breakfast requires any cooking at all, the utensil you probably reach for nine times out of ten is a frying pan or skillet.

Whatever you call this utensil, it is useful to know some of the characteristics that enable a frying pan to perform well. The choices in materials and design in today's frying pans can be a little bewildering. If you are in the market for a new one, here are some tips that can help you decide.

The single most important factor in choosing a good frying pan is its weight. A simple rule is to select the heaviest one you can handle easily. The heavier the pan, the better and more evenly it will hold and conduct heat and the less likely it is to warp or buckle with long use.

Consider also the balance of a prospective frying pan. It should sit evenly on the cooking surface and not be tipped askew by a handle that is too heavy. Heft it—the design of the handle should permit you to lift and tilt the pan skillfully.

How well a frying pan conducts heat depends in large part on the substance from which it is made. *Copper* is the best heat conductor for surface cooking, and a heavy French copper skillet is the first choice of many food cooks. Quality copper pans are esteemed because of their beauty and durability—they last forever and can be handed down to the next generation. And when you cook with copper, you use relatively low heat, saving fuel.

On the minus side, however, copper pans are usually lined with tin, which must be replaced in time. An idea that sounds extravagant—replacing the tin lining with silver—may be practical when one considers the greater durability of silver over the life of the pan. Of course, both copper and silver require frequent polishing to look their best.

Considerably less costly—and with as many partisans as a material for the perfect frying pan—is *iron*. It is used in two quite different forms: *Rolled steel* is the lighter-weight material and is often seen in omelet and crêpe pans; *cast iron* is much heavier and may be unfinished or coated with porcelain enamel. All forms conduct heat well. Both rolled steel and uncoated cast iron pans must be seasoned often with oil and kept in a dry place to remain rust free.

To season a pan of this sort, first scrub it with fine steel wool and wash it well. Then coat the inside generously with a flavorless vegetable oil (preferably not safflower oil). Place the pan over medium heat and heat it until the fat begins to smoke. Remove the pan from the heat and let it cool completely; then use paper towels to wipe out the excess oil. After seasoning, the pan—especially an omelet pan—should never be washed. Simply wipe it clean with a paper towel and a little oil after use. From time to time, you may need to repeat the seasoning process.

Some enameled cast iron frying pans have a dark, nonstick coating applied by the manufacturer. It is designed for high-temperature cooking. For this and other special finishes, it is a good idea to follow the manufacturer's directions for seasoning or otherwise preparing the pan before using it for cooking. Read the label or accompanying literature.

Cast iron is not as indestructible as its weight might suggest. If dropped on a hard surface, it may crack or break. It is also too heavy for many people to handle without a struggle.

Aluminum is another material that makes a fine frying pan. Aluminum pans come in many forms. *Spun aluminum* frying pans in classic French shapes, especially omelet pans, are versatile. One can also find a handsome variety of *cast aluminum* skillets. In all its forms aluminum is a good conductor of heat, but it is rather soft; abrasive cleaners should be used cautiously. Because aluminum is lightweight, it can be used to make a pan that is thick enough to hold heat well, but that is so light that it handles easily.

Special finishes have improved aluminum cookware in the past several years. Developed for professional cooks, Calphalon cookware with its smooth, dark, fused-on coating will not discolor or react chemically with food and resists sticking.

A different sort of finish is Du-Pont's durable new SilverStone non-stick coating, which is fused onto the pan material. You will find it on the aluminum frying pans of many manufacturers. Be sure the pan beneath is worthy of the coating. For many years of dependable use, choose a well-constructed pan that is substantial enough not to warp.

Finally, there is *stainless steel.* In spite of its good looks, this material has long had a bad name among serious cooks. Stainless steel is known to be a poor conductor, with hot spots where food sticks or burns. If you insist on using it, look for a stainless steel pan with a bottom containing a thick core of some other metal with better heat-conducting properties—copper or aluminum.

Regardless of the material you select, for all-around breakfast cooking you will probably want frying pans of at least two different sizes. For omelets, experienced cooks say an 8-inch-diameter pan is the most useful. A 10- to 12-inch frying pan is a good size for other preparations—scrambling or frying eggs, sautéeing bacon or sausages, and many others. The pans shown in this photo are, clockwise from upper left, of Calphalon, SilverStone coating on aluminum, enameled cast iron, cast aluminum, stainless steel, and cast iron. At the center is a copper pan.

Enjoy a leisurely brunch of Fresh Spinach and Mushroom Omelet (page 52), Cheddar Cheese Muffins (page 113), and Orange Batter Bread (page 119).

Whether freshly squeezed or made from concentrate, orange juice makes a great eye-opening beverage any time of the day.

Beverages

Waking up to the fragrance of good coffee brewing is one of life's small delights. Mingled with morning sunshine, the smell of fine coffee seems to carry the promise of the day's possibilities. For those who prefer to sip something other than coffee in the morning, the alternatives are many: Frothy hot chocolate or a well-made cup of sturdy breakfast tea each have many devotees; fresh fruit juices are nutritious eye-openers. And for brunch, one can begin with the elegance of chilled Champagne, a creamy gin fizz, or a brisk Bloody Mary.

Faster than fast food—try a bit of fruit, some robust espresso, and a Fried Egg Muffin Sandwich (page 44) for a quick and easy pick-me-up breakfast.

COFFEE

If you judged coffee only by the convincingly enacted scenarios of television commercials, you could easily believe that a great cup of coffee starts with a jar of instant coffee or a vacuum-packed can of ground coffee from the supermarket. But if your taste in coffee is more critical, it's clear that this is only the beginning of the coffee story.

The proliferation of shops specializing in coffees from all over the world attests to a growing interest in fine coffee. Sold as whole beans or ground to order, such coffees are also available in a variety of roasts, in any quantity you like.

If exploring coffee is new to you, you may wish to try just a small amount of several types—say ¼ pound. When you find your favorite, then purchase a larger quantity. The flavor of coffee is affected in part by its origin: Coffee-producing areas include high-altitude regions of several South American, Caribbean, and African nations.

Roasting develops the flavor of coffee and determines the darkness and shininess of the beans. Darker roasts are popular for after-dinner coffee and for breakfast coffee that will be mixed with a quantity of hot milk. Of these, Vienna roast is the lightest, and French and Italian, or espresso, roast are the darkest.

Freshness is one of the most critical factors in brewing a fine cup of coffee. Ground coffee loses flavor quickly, and that is why many connoisseurs buy whole coffee beans and grind them just before brewing each pot. Store coffee, tightly covered, in a dark, cool place. If you buy coffee in large amounts, package the bulk of it airtight and store it in the freezer. Then remove small amounts as needed. The usual proportion is 2 tablespoons ground coffee for each 8-ounce cup.

The method of brewing is also important. Most experts favor a filter-type drip pot because it removes the brewed coffee fairly quickly from the grounds, and because the coffee can be made with water just below the boiling point—overly high heat is the enemy of good coffee flavor. The French have a saying, *"Café bouilli, café foutu"* (If it boils, it's killed).

And, of course, the pot should be sparkling clean: Any residue of oily coffee film lingering in the pot may contribute an unpleasant flavor. Unusual coffeepots for making special kinds of coffee are discussed in the Special Feature on page 15.

SPECIAL POTS FOR SPECIAL COFFEE

If you really enjoy fine coffee, the day will come when your standard, everyday coffee maker is no longer enough. Here are just some of the varieties from a world tour of coffee-appreciating countries.

The Turkish or Middle Eastern *ibrik* represents one of the earliest ways of brewing coffee. Often made of gleaming copper trimmed with brass, it looks like an oversized butter warmer. (Its shape resembles a bell, open at the top.) Making coffee in an ibrik is quite unsophisticated—one just pours boiling water over very finely ground dark-roast coffee and stirs until it reaches the desired strength. Some people describe coffee of this type as being so strong it is actually *thick*. It is usually served heavily sweetened.

From France comes the idea of the *plunger-type* coffeepot or *cafetière*. It consists of a clear glass carafe that is fitted into a metal or plastic frame.

To use it, place finely ground dark-roast coffee in the bottom, and pour in hot water to the top of the frame. Let the mixture stand to infuse for about five minutes, then insert the snug-fitting plunger and slowly press the mesh screen filter down to the bottom. This process separates the coffee from the grounds, and it is now ready to drink.

Another French pot is the three-part *porcelain drip* coffee maker. It works much like other drip pots—coarsely ground coffee is placed in the upper portion, and hot water is poured through to drip through the grounds and into the lower part.

Italy is renowned for *espresso*, coffee brewed with steam. Although many costly electric espresso makers are available, less expensive stove-top espresso pots also produce a fairly authentic demitasse of the dark, fragrant brew.

The simplest espresso pot is a three-piece, hourglass-shaped affair of polished or satin-finish aluminum. Water goes in the lower pot, finely ground coffee in a basket in the middle. When the water boils, steam rises through the coffee and condenses in the upper container, where the pouring spout is located.

A more elaborate version of the espresso pot consists of side-by-side containers connected by a hollow overhead bridge. Water is placed in one side, coffee in a basket over an empty metal pitcher in the other. The principle is similar to that of the hourglass-shaped pot: As the water boils, steam is forced through the coffee to condense in the pitcher. Some espresso makers have a jet that, when opened, emits steam to heat milk for *cappuccino*.

Another style of Italian coffeepot is a three-piece, drip-filter arrangement that stacks to make a tall cylinder with handles. It is called a *macchinetta* or *napoletana*. Place water in the bottom pot and coffee in the perforated filter basket in the center. When the water boils, the pot is turned over, and the water drips through the coffee into the empty container with the pouring spout. Shown above are, clockwise from left, a porcelain drip pot, an hourglass espresso pot, a side-by-side espresso pot, an ibrik, a macchinetta, and a cafetière.

15

Give your day international excitement with French pastries and a bracing cup of strong French-style coffee. Instructions for using special coffee pots are on page 15. The recipe and tips for making these Croissants are on page 121.

CAFÉ AU LAIT

Breakfast in France has more substance than one might think, thanks to the amount of rich, steaming milk that is poured into those oversized coffee cups in which café au lait is served. It may be the flakiness of the croissant that you remember, but it's the protein of the milk that keeps you going until restaurants open for lunch at half-past noon.

> 1 cup milk
> 2 cups strong, hot, dark-roast coffee
> Sugar (optional)

1. Pour milk into a small saucepan. Place over medium heat until milk is steaming hot but just under the boiling point. Pour into a warm pitcher.

2. Fill large coffee cups or mugs two-thirds full of hot coffee. Add hot milk, stirring to blend. Add sugar to taste, if desired.

Serves 2 to 3.

CAFFÈ LATTÈ

The Italian interpretation of café au lait is made with hot milk frothy with steam created by an espresso pot with a steam jet—sometimes called a cappuccino pot. The only real difference between caffè lattè and cappuccino is the size of the cup; cappuccino is served in a smaller one.

> 2 cups milk
> 2 cups hot espresso coffee
> Ground cinnamon or powdered, sweetened cocoa
> Sugar (optional)

1. Using steam from an espresso coffee maker, heat milk in a deep, heatproof container until frothy. Pour most of the milk, reserving a little of the foam, into 4 tall, heatproof mugs.

2. Slowly pour coffee down sides of mugs. Spoon reserved milk foam over coffee. Sprinkle lightly with cinnamon.

3. Serve with spoons. Add sugar to taste, if desired.

Serves 4.

IRISH COFFEE

Too rich for all but the most opulent breakfasts, Irish coffee might be served as a sort of dessert-in-a-glass to cap a winter brunch.

> 8 sugar lumps (½-in. square)
> 3 cups strong, hot coffee
> 6 ounces (¾ cup) Irish whiskey
> Slightly whipped cream

1. Rinse 4 heatproof 8-ounce footed glasses or mugs with hot water and drain quickly.

2. Place 2 lumps sugar in each glass. Add ¾ cup steaming hot coffee and 1½ ounces (3 tbsp) Irish whiskey to each. Stir well to dissolve sugar.

3. Top each with a dollop of cream, and serve at once.

Serves 4.

Spicy Hot Chocolate, New Mexico Style (page 18) warms a breakfast of fresh oranges and sweet rolls. Pastry recipes begin on page 110.

BREAKFAST TEA

A fine pot of tea in the morning has many enthusiasts. Browse among the teas your favorite coffee-and-tea shop sells and you will find some designated "breakfast tea," both English and Irish. (The English is usually heartier in flavor.) But any medium- to rich-bodied blend of black tea you enjoy can hit the spot in the morning.

Making a good cup of tea requires attention to a few simple rules. First warm the pot (an earthenware one, preferably) by filling it with hot water; set it aside while the kettle boils. Measure a teaspoon of tea for each 8-ounce cup. If you wish, place the tea leaves in a perforated tea ball or infuser for easy removal.

Place tea and boiling water in the warm pot, and let the tea steep for 4½ to 5 minutes; then pour the tea (through a strainer if tea was placed loose in pot) at once. Some grandmotherly advice that holds up well: If you want stronger tea, use *more* tea—longer brewing only makes the tea taste bitter.

ORANGE SPICED TEA

Here is a pleasantly flavored blend of tea with citrus and spices to keep on hand for a bit of variety at breakfast or brunch.

> ½ cup loose black tea leaves
> 1 stick (2 to 3 in.) cinnamon, broken into 3 or 4 pieces
> ¼ teaspoon each *whole allspice and whole cloves*
> ⅛ teaspoon ground ginger
> 2 pods whole cardamom, slightly crushed
> 1 strip (2 in.) lemon rind
> 2 teaspoons grated orange rind

1. Combine all ingredients in a covered jar, then let stand at room temperature 2 to 3 days before using.

2. Brew as for unflavored tea, following procedure above.

Makes about ½ cup flavored tea mixture.

HOT CHOCOLATE

In the 1500s, chocolate drinks were as much a sensation as coffee would be a century later.

HOT CHOCOLATE, NEW MEXICO STYLE

From the American Southwest, comes hot chocolate flavored with spices.

> ¼ cup each *sugar and unsweetened cocoa*
> ½ teaspoon instant coffee powder or granules
> ⅛ teaspoon salt
> 1 cup water
> 1 stick (2 to 3 in.) cinnamon
> 2 cups milk
> 1 cup half-and-half
> 1 tablespoon vanilla extract
> ⅛ teaspoon ground cloves

1. In a 2- to 3-quart saucepan mix sugar, cocoa, instant coffee, and salt. Stir in water; add cinnamon stick. Bring to a boil, reduce heat, and simmer for 5 minutes.

2. Add milk and half-and-half to cocoa mixture, stirring constantly. Bring to a boil and then remove from heat.

3. Mix in vanilla and cloves; remove cinnamon stick; beat until foamy, then serve.

Serves 4 to 6.

DOUBLE MOCHA

This luscious hot drink makes a brunch treat with brioches or other homemade bread and fresh fruit.

> 2½ tablespoons unsweetened cocoa
> ¼ cup sugar
>   Dash salt
> ¼ cup hot water
> 2 cups milk
> ¼ teaspoon vanilla extract
> 2 cups hot espresso coffee
>   Whipped cream (optional)

1. In a medium saucepan stir together cocoa, sugar, and salt. Blend in water. Bring to a boil over medium heat, stirring constantly for 1 minute.

2. Gradually add milk, stirring with a whisk. Heat until cocoa is steaming hot but just under the boiling point. Add vanilla, then beat with whisk until cocoa is frothy. Pour into mugs, filling them half full.

3. Fill mugs with espresso. Top each with a dollop of whipped cream, if desired.

Serves 4 to 6.

ECSTATICALLY RICH HOT CHOCOLATE

Inspired by the legendary hot chocolate of the French Basque port city of Bayonne, this foamy cup is made with a combination of unsweetened and semisweet chocolate. Amaretto transforms it into an Italian treat.

> 2 ounces (2 squares) each *semisweet chocolate and unsweetened chocolate, coarsely chopped*
> ⅓ cup granulated sugar
> 2 tablespoons brown sugar
> 2 cups each *milk and half-and-half*
> ½ teaspoon vanilla extract

1. In a 2-quart saucepan combine chocolate, sugars, milk, and half-and-half. Place over medium heat, stirring frequently with a whisk until chocolate melts, sugar dissolves, and mixture is steaming hot but just under the boiling point. Reduce heat to keep chocolate hot.

2. Pour about half of the hot chocolate into a blender and whirl until frothy; stir into remaining hot chocolate in pan.

3. Mix in vanilla and serve at once.

Serves 4 to 6.

Hot Chocolate Amaretto Prepare Ecstatically Rich Hot Chocolate, omitting vanilla. Into each serving stir 1 tablespoon amaretto liqueur.

BREAKFAST-IN-A-GLASS

Fresh Fruit Blender Drink

Egg Bread
Cinnamon Toast

Coffee

Even when time is short, you needn't let it stop you from enjoying a wholesome breakfast. Any of the blender drinks that follow can be whirled together in a jiffy, but are satisfying enough to keep you going all morning.

Try each of the three flavors—then you will be able to use the same principle to put together your own breakfast creations. Hot cinnamon toast and a cup of coffee are nice additions to the basic breakfast, if time permits.

NECTARINE-PLUM DRINK

- 1 unpeeled nectarine, pitted and coarsely chopped
- 1 unpeeled plum, pitted and coarsely chopped
- 1 teaspoon lemon juice
- 1 egg
- 1 cup milk
- 1 tablespoon Vanilla Sugar (see page 30)
  Pinch ground nutmeg

1. Place all ingredients in blender. Whirl until smooth.

2. Serve at once, with a straw.

Serves 1.

FRESH STRAWBERRY DRINK

- ½ cup hulled, halved strawberries
- 2 teaspoons lemon juice
- 2 tablespoons Vanilla Sugar (see page 30)
- 1 egg
- ½ cup each *plain yogurt and milk*

1. Place all ingredients in blender. Whirl until smooth.

2. Serve at once, with a straw.

Serves 1.

BANANA-LEMON DRINK

- 1 banana, peeled and cut in chunks
- 1 egg
- 1 tablespoon lemon juice
- ½ teaspoon grated lemon rind
- ½ cup each *plain yogurt and milk*
- 1½ teaspoons Vanilla Sugar (see page 30)
  Pinch each *ground cinnamon and nutmeg*

1. Place all ingredients in blender. Whirl until smooth.

2. Serve at once, with a straw.

Serves 1.

19

Warm up a winter get-together with Hot Spiced Cider. Great by itself or with pastries, it is shown here with Banana-Nut Coffee Cake (page 115).

FRUIT JUICES

Most people enjoy fruit in some form in the morning. When there isn't time to sit down to a half grapefruit or a bowl of cut fruit, a glass of bottled orange or tomato juice is a quick and healthy substitute. Better still are freshly squeezed citrus juices, singly or in combination.

WINTER CITRUS WAKE-UP

Blending fruit juices results in some refreshing mixtures. Try this one: orange juice whirled with pink grapefruit and lime juice. The tart edge is bound to banish any morning grogginess.

> 4 oranges
> 1 pink grapefruit
> 1 lime

1. Cut fruits in halves crosswise, and squeeze juices from them with a reamer or an electric juicer.

2. Strain juices into blender or cocktail shaker. Whirl or shake until foamy and well blended. Cover and refrigerate if made ahead, then shake well before serving.

Serves 3 to 4.

PINK FRUIT JUICE FROTH

For a special occasion, pour this melon-pink fruit juice medley to drink through straws.

> 1 basket (about 2 cups) strawberries, hulled
> 1 cup seeded, diced watermelon
> Juice of 2 oranges
> Juice of 1 lime
> 1 to 2 tablespoons sugar

1. In blender or food processor combine strawberries, watermelon, and orange and lime juices. Whirl or process until smooth and well blended.

2. Add sugar to taste. Cover and refrigerate if made ahead.

3. Serve each drink with a straw.

Serves 4.

HOT SPICED CIDER

A pan of this fragrant brew kept warm on an electric warmer or over a candle will perfume a winter brunch. It is delicious with homemade doughnuts or quick coffee cake.

> 2 tablespoons brown sugar
> 1 teaspoon grated fresh ginger or ¼ teaspoon ground ginger
> ¼ teaspoon whole allspice
> 5 whole cloves
> 1 3-inch strip lemon rind
> 1 stick (2 to 3 in.) cinnamon
> 4 cups cider or apple juice

1. In a 2-quart saucepan combine brown sugar, ginger, allspice, cloves, lemon rind, and cinnamon stick.

2. Add cider and place over medium heat, stirring until sugar dissolves and mixture begins to boil. Cover, reduce heat, and simmer for 5 to 10 minutes to blend flavors.

3. Strain into heatproof mugs or cups.

Serves 4 to 6.

Four fruits blend together smoothly to make Pink Fruit Juice Froth. Use a blender or food processor for this vitamin-packed and appealing morning treat. It's also delicious as an afternoon pick-me-up.

Brunch Italian style combines Italian Jam-Filled Crescents (page 124) and a Bellini (page 24)—an apéritif that combines sparkling wine with fresh white peaches.

2 cups water
½ cup each *sugar and raisins*
1 *lemon, thinly sliced*
1 *stick (2 to 3 in.) cinnamon*
1 *teaspoon whole cloves*
2 *whole pods cardamom, split*
6 cups (48 oz) *cranberry juice cocktail*
1½ cups *freshly squeezed tangerine or tangelo juice*
   Whole blanched almonds

1. In a 3- to 4-quart saucepan combine water, sugar, raisins, lemon, cinnamon stick, cloves, and cardamom. Bring to a boil, stirring until sugar is dissolved, then reduce heat and simmer, uncovered, for 5 minutes.

2. Add cranberry juice and tangerine juice. Heat, stirring occasionally, until mixture is steaming hot, but do not let it boil.

3. Place an almond in each heat-proof mug or cup and strain hot punch over it.

Serves 10 to 12.

CHAMPAGNE AND OTHER BRUNCH DRINKS

A sparkling wine makes a festivity of any breakfast or brunch. Still wines also complement many brunch menus: White or rosé wines are usually favored for their lightness.

You will wish to choose wines to enhance the specific dishes that make up your menu, of course. But brunch foods often lend themselves to the company of such fruity white wines as Chenin Blanc, Gewürztraminer, Gray Riesling, and Sauvignon Blanc. Have a look, also, at some of the blushing white wines made from red wine grapes—"white" Pinot Noir, Zinfandel, Cabernet, and so forth.

HOT MULLED CRANBERRY PUNCH

It has the crimson color of mulled wine and the spicy seasonings that flavor Swedish *glögg*—but this festive punch is a nonalcoholic fruit juice combination. To spike it, add a tablespoon or two of brandy to each mug before straining in the punch.

MIMOSA

Fresh orange juice and Champagne, accented by an orange-flavored liqueur, combine to make the delicate brunch classic, the Mimosa.

1 cup freshly squeezed
    orange juice
¼ cup orange-flavored liqueur
1 bottle (750 ml) chilled brut
    or extra-dry Champagne

1. Divide orange juice and orange-flavored liqueur evenly into each of 4 to 6 wine glasses.

2. Fill slowly with Champagne, mixing lightly to blend. Serve at once.

Serves 4 to 6.

HAZEL'S RAMOS GIN FIZZ

Creamy drinks such as this gin fizz are always popular at brunch.

1 cup cold half-and-half
½ cup gin
¼ to ⅓ cup confectioners' sugar
2 egg whites
½ teaspoon orange flower water
1 cup crushed ice
    Juice of 1 lemon (3 to 4 tbsp)

1. In blender combine half-and-half, gin, confectioners' sugar, egg whites, and orange flower water. Add ice and lemon juice.

2. Blend at high speed until very foamy. Serve at once.

Serves 4.

A blender makes quick work of these traditional brunch drinks: a Piña Colada, a Tequila Sunrise, and a Strawberry Daiquiri (all on page 24). Garnish the glasses with fruit for a professional presentation.

SPIRITED MILK PUNCH

Traditional for New Year's Day is this frothy milk punch.

- 1 cup brandy or whiskey
- 2 cups cold milk
- ¼ cup confectioners' sugar
- ½ teaspoon vanilla extract
- ½ cup crushed ice
  Freshly grated nutmeg

1. In blender combine brandy, milk, confectioners' sugar, vanilla, and ice. Whirl until frothy and well combined.

2. Pour into wine glasses or punch cups. Grate nutmeg over each serving.

Serves 4 to 6.

BELLINI

Made with the juice of fresh white-fleshed peaches, the Bellini is a creation of Harry's Bar in Venice. It should be made with Prosecco, a sparkling wine from the Veneto region, to be authentic. However, Asti spumante is more widely exported and also produces an elegant drink.

- 2 medium-sized white peaches (such as Babcock, Springtime, or Pat's Pride)
- 1 tablespoon sugar
- 1 teaspoon powdered ascorbic acid
- 2 teaspoons lemon juice
- 2 bottles (750 ml each) chilled Prosecco or Asti spumante

1. Peel, pit, and coarsely chop peaches. Place in food processor or blender with sugar, ascorbic acid, and lemon juice. Process or whirl until smooth.

2. Strain peach mixture into a small bowl; cover and refrigerate if made ahead.

3. Pour Prosecco into 6- to 8-ounce wine glasses, filling them about half full. To each glass add about 1 tablespoon peach mixture and stir carefully to blend. Add more Prosecco to almost fill glasses. Serve at once.

Serves 12.

STRAWBERRY DAIQUIRI

You can make this pretty drink even when fresh strawberries are not in the market—it's done with frozen berries. The drink also has a spirited variation—Banana Daiquiri.

- 1 egg white
  Sugar
- 1 package (16 oz) frozen unsweetened strawberries, partially thawed
- 1 cup light rum
- 2 tablespoons lemon juice
- 6 tablespoons sugar
- 1 cup crushed ice
  Whole strawberries, for garnish (optional)

1. To frost glasses, beat egg white in a small bowl until it begins to froth. Dip rims of glasses first in egg white, then in sugar. Set aside until frosted rims are set.

2. In blender combine strawberries, rum, lemon juice, the 6 tablespoons sugar, and ice. Whirl at high speed until frothy and well combined.

3. Pour into frosted glasses and serve at once, garnishing each drink with a strawberry, if desired. Serve with straws.

Serves 4 to 6.

Banana Daiquiri In place of strawberries use 2 medium bananas. Substitute ¼ cup lime juice for the lemon juice. Use only 2 tablespoons sugar. Omit strawberry garnish.

PIÑA COLADA

A favorite among the creamy drinks made in the blender is this tropical-flavored combination of rum, coconut cream, and pineapple juice.

- 1 cup light rum
- ¾ cup canned cream of coconut (sweetened)
- 1½ cups pineapple juice
- ½ cup half-and-half
- 1 cup crushed ice
  Pineapple slices or spears, for garnish

1. In blender combine rum, coconut cream, pineapple juice, half-and-half, and ice.

2. Whirl at high speed until frothy and well combined.

3. Pour into 4 tall, footed or stemmed glasses. Garnish each with a pineapple slice.

Serves 4.

TEQUILA SUNRISE

The tropical flavors of this handsome, tall drink make it a good choice to precede or accompany a brunch with a south-of-the-border or Hawaiian theme.

- ¼ cup grenadine syrup
- ¾ cup tequila
- 2 cups cold orange juice
- ¼ cup orange-flavored liqueur
- 2 cups crushed ice
  Orange slices, for garnish

1. Divide grenadine equally into each of 4 tall, footed or stemmed glasses.

2. In blender combine tequila, orange juice, liqueur, and ice. Whirl at high speed briefly, just until all ingredients are well combined.

3. Pour tequila mixture slowly into glasses (to keep the grenadine layer intact). Garnish each drink with an orange slice. Serve at once with straws.

Serves 4.

SANGRIA

If your brunch has a Mexican accent—*enchiladas* or *huevos rancheros*, for example—a pitcher of fruity red wine is a fine companion.

> *Juice of 1 orange*
> *Juice of 2 lemons*
> *Juice of 1 lime*
> ⅓ *cup sugar*
> ¼ *cup orange-flavored liqueur*
> 1 *bottle (750 ml) dry red wine*
> *Orange, lemon, lime, and strawberry slices*
> 1 *quart chilled club soda*

1. In a 2½- to 3-quart pitcher or a punch bowl, stir together orange juice, lemon juice, lime juice, sugar, and liqueur, mixing until sugar is dissolved. Mix in wine, then orange, lemon, lime, and strawberry slices to taste. Cover and refrigerate for 3 to 4 hours.

2. To serve, mix in club soda. Pour over ice in large wine glasses.

Serves 6 to 8.

BLOODY MARY

When you are serving a number of people, it is handy to have a blenderful of the seasoned tomato juice base in readiness to stir up this popular, tall vodka drink.

> 3 *cups cold tomato juice*
> ¼ *cup lemon juice*
> 1 *teaspoon each salt and Worcestershire sauce*
> ¼ *teaspoon each hot-pepper sauce and prepared horseradish*
> *Pinch freshly ground pepper*
> ¾ *cup vodka*
> *Ice cubes (optional)*
> 4 *celery sticks, for garnish*

1. In blender combine tomato juice, lemon juice, salt, Worcestershire sauce, hot-pepper sauce, horseradish, and pepper. Whirl until well combined.

2. Pour vodka into 4 tall, slender glasses, using 3 tablespoons for each drink. Add ice cubes, if desired. Then divide tomato juice mixture among the glasses and stir well. Garnish each drink with a celery stick.

Serves 4.

Instead of using a bottled mix, add your own fresh seasonings for an especially vigorous Bloody Mary. For a garnish variation, try a lime quarter, cucumber spear, or whole green bean.

There are luscious fruits available during every season, but these summertime berries perhaps best capture the essence of appetizing freshness.

Fruits

The color and fragrance of fresh fruit brightens the morning. Fruits are also rich repositories of a host of necessary nutrients. Apricots abound in a substance the body uses to make vitamin A (which helps to fight colds and other infections and prevents night blindness). Citrus fruits and strawberries contain vitamin C (which promotes healing and may have a role in preventing colds). Melons are a good source of both vitamins A and C. The body can store vitamin A, but not vitamin C, so a food rich in the latter is needed every day for good health.

SEASONAL FRUIT

There is nothing like fresh fruit to complete any breakfast or brunch. It adds special color, texture, and flavor to any type of morning meal. For a weekday breakfast it may just be a matter of slicing a banana over your corn flakes or treating yourself to a small dish of perfect berries. For a brunch, fruit can serve two purposes: a refreshing opener to the repast or an elegant dessert. Consider centering your buffet table with a glass bowl glowing with multicolored fruits. The Four Seasons Fresh Fruit Bowl, featured in these four photographs, consists of a basic theme with variations—luscious seasonal fruit changes and highlights the basic mixture, providing you with four recipes in one. The basic mix is made up of oranges, apples, and bananas, which are available in most areas throughout the year. The caption lists the ingredients for each season. The recipe is on page 30.

28

Use oranges, apples, and bananas as a basic mix for each variation of the Four Seasons Fresh Fruit Bowl featured on the next page. In winter (upper left), add a pear, pineapple, papaya, and some lime juice. In spring (lower left), add strawberries and kiwi fruit. For the summer fruit bowl (upper right) choose nectarines, peaches, seedless grapes, cherries, and berries. And for a fall fruit mix (lower right), add red grapes, Bartlett pears, and a shower of crimson pomegranate seeds.

FOUR SEASONS FRESH FRUIT BOWL

Starting with fruits you can find the year around—oranges, apples, and bananas—add fruits of the season to make a generous help-yourself fruit bowl at any time.

3 oranges
2 unpeeled tart red apples, cored and diced
2 firm-ripe bananas, sliced about ½ inch thick
1 tablespoon lemon juice

Seasonal Fruits

Fresh fruits (see below)

Vanilla Sugar

Half a vanilla bean
½ cup sugar

1. Working over a large bowl, peel oranges close to fruit, cutting away the bitter, white inner peel. Using a sharp paring knife, cut close to membranes, removing juicy segments of fruit and placing in bowl.

2. Add apples, bananas, and lemon juice; mix lightly. Gently mix in Seasonal Fruits. If made ahead, cover and refrigerate until ready to serve, up to 3 hours.

3. Sweeten to taste with Vanilla Sugar.

Serves 6 to 8.

Seasonal Fruits For *spring*, add 2 cups (1 basket) strawberries (hulled and cut in halves if large) and 2 kiwi fruit (peeled and sliced about ¼ inch thick).

For *summer*, add 2 nectarines or peaches (peeled if you wish, pitted, and sliced) and ½ cup *each* seedless red or green grapes; blueberries, blackberries, or raspberries; pitted sweet cherries; and diced cantaloupe or honeydew melon.

For *fall*, add 1 cup halved, seeded red grapes; 2 Bartlett pears (peeled, cored, and diced); and ¼ cup pomegranate seeds.

For *winter*, add 1 winter pear (Anjou, Bosc, or Comice), peeled, cored, and diced; 1 cup peeled, cored, diced fresh pineapple; and 1 cup peeled, seeded, diced papaya. Substitute lime juice for lemon juice if you wish.

Vanilla Sugar Embed half a vanilla bean in sugar in a covered jar for at least 24 hours. Replenish sugar as you use Vanilla Sugar to sweeten fruits.

BROILED PINK GRAPEFRUIT

A mixture of butter, brown sugar, and a touch of nutmeg gilds juicy pink grapefruit.

3 pink grapefruit
¼ cup butter or margarine, softened
¼ cup firmly packed light brown sugar
⅛ teaspoon ground nutmeg

1. Preheat broiler. Cut grapefruit in halves. Using a grapefruit knife, loosen fruit from skin around edges and between segments. Discard seeds. Place grapefruit, cut sides up, in a shallow-rimmed baking pan.

2. In a small bowl beat together butter, brown sugar, and nutmeg until smooth and well combined. Dot butter mixture evenly over the grapefruit halves.

3. Place beneath broiler, about 4 inches from heat. Broil until topping is melted, bubbling, and lightly browned (3 to 5 minutes). Serve hot.

Serves 6.

ELEGANT ORANGES

Another way of beginning or ending a brunch is with slices of lightly spiced oranges drizzled with an orange-flavored liqueur.

4 medium oranges
1 tablespoon sugar, mixed with ¼ teaspoon ground cinnamon
2 tablespoons orange-flavored liqueur

1. Working over a wide, shallow bowl, peel oranges close to fruit, cutting away the bitter, white inner peel. Thinly slice oranges crosswise, removing any seeds. Spread orange slices in bowl.

2. Sprinkle evenly with sugar-and-cinnamon mixture, then with liqueur.

3. Let oranges stand, uncovered, at room temperature for 30 minutes to an hour before serving in small bowls with juices spooned over.

Serves 4 to 6.

HOT BUTTERED PLUMS

These fresh summer plums in a tart orange sauce are nice to serve from a chafing dish, either alone or as a topping for crêpes or crisp waffles.

¼ cup butter or margarine
½ cup sugar
2 teaspoons cornstarch
⅛ teaspoon ground nutmeg
4 cups quartered, pitted red plums
½ teaspoon vanilla extract
Juice and grated rind of 1 small orange

1. In a large frying pan, melt butter over medium heat. Stir in sugar, cornstarch, and nutmeg. Mix in plums, turning to coat with sugar mixture. Cook, stirring occasionally, until juices form a thick sauce (3 to 5 minutes).

2. Remove from heat; gently stir in vanilla and orange juice and rind. Return to heat and stir until sauce boils and thickens slightly (2 to 3 minutes). Serve hot.

Serves 6.

PEACHES AND BLUEBERRIES WITH CREAM

Two summer favorites make a handsome combination to serve with cream or to spoon over a puffy oven pancake (see page 94).

    4 large peaches
    2 tablespoons lemon juice
    1 cup fresh or frozen
       (unsweetened) blueberries
    ¼ cup sugar
    ⅛ teaspoon ground nutmeg
    1 teaspoon grated lemon rind
       Whipping cream or
       half-and-half

1. To peel peaches, half-fill a large saucepan with hot water, bring to a boil, and add peaches, 2 at a time. Boil each batch for 30 seconds, then remove peaches and rinse with cold water. Use a small knife to carefully slip off skins.

2. Slice peaches thinly (you should have about 5 cups); place in a medium bowl and mix lightly with lemon juice and blueberries. In a small bowl mix sugar, nutmeg, and lemon rind. Add sugar mixture to peach mixture, and mix lightly. Let stand for about 30 minutes before serving.

3. Spoon peach mixture into bowls. Pass a pitcher of cream to pour over peaches to taste.

Serves 6.

MELON BALLS SPUMANTE

Bubbly with a delicate Italian wine, this fruit medley can be served to open a brunch or as a light dessert with crisp cookies.

    4 cups each 1-inch seeded
       Persian melon or cantaloupe
       and honeydew melon balls
    2 teaspoons lemon juice
       Pinch freshly grated nutmeg
    1 cup chilled Asti spumante

1. In a glass serving bowl lightly mix melon, lemon juice, and nutmeg.

2. Slowly pour in Asti spumante; mix lightly. Serve at once, or cover and refrigerate for up to 2 hours.

3. Place melon into individual serving dishes, spooning liquid over.

Serves 6 to 8.

Serve Melon Balls Spumante in place of a salad to open a meal or joined with cookies and sparkling wine, as an elegant grand finale.

CHUNKY SAUTÉED APPLES WITH LEMON

For an out-of-the-ordinary family breakfast some winter weekend, bake gingerbread and serve it warm with this tart-sweet applesauce.

- 2 tablespoons butter
- 5 medium-sized tart cooking apples, peeled and cut in bite-sized chunks
- 1 teaspoon grated lemon rind
- 1 tablespoon lemon juice
- ⅛ teaspoon ground nutmeg
- ½ cup sugar
- 2 tablespoons pear brandy (optional)

1. Heat butter in a large frying pan over moderately high heat until foamy. Mix in apples, lemon rind, lemon juice, and nutmeg. Cook, uncovered, stirring occasionally, until apples are almost tender (8 to 10 minutes).

2. Stir in sugar and cook, stirring gently, for about 2 minutes longer, until apples are tender to your taste. Mix in pear brandy (if used) and cook, stirring, until most of the liquid is reduced.

3. Serve warm, at room temperature, or chilled.

Serves 4 to 6.

CINNAMON-PINK APPLESAUCE

Tiny red cinnamon candies give this homemade applesauce a spicy tang and hot pink color.

- 6 medium-sized (about 2 lbs) tart cooking apples, peeled, cored, and cut in chunks
- ¼ cup sugar
- 2 tablespoons tiny red-hot cinnamon candies
- ¼ cup water

1. Place apples in a 2-quart saucepan with sugar, cinnamon candies, and water.

2. Bring to a boil, cover, reduce heat, and cook, stirring occasionally, until apples are very tender (15 to 20 minutes).

3. Stir with a fork until mixture has a saucelike consistency. (Put through a food mill or process until smooth in a food processor if you wish.)

4. Serve warm, at room temperature, or chilled.

Serves 6.

WINTER FRUIT COMPOTE

These dried fruits, plumped in spiced port, make a handsome combination. Enjoy them—cooked the night before—while a Sunday morning quiche bakes.

- ½ pound (about 1¼ cup) dried prunes
- 1 package (6 oz) dried apricots
- 1 stick (2 to 3 in.) cinnamon Half a lemon, thinly sliced Juice of 1 orange
- 3 tablespoons brown sugar Water
- ¼ cup port wine

1. In a 2-quart saucepan combine prunes, apricots, cinnamon stick, lemon slices, and orange juice. Sprinkle with brown sugar. Add just enough water to barely cover fruits.

2. Bring to a boil, cover, reduce heat, and simmer until fruits are plump and tender (8 to 10 minutes).

3. Stir in port; transfer to a glass bowl. Serve fruits (with their liquid) warm, at room temperature, or chilled.

Serves 6.

SPICED RHUBARB

Pink stalks of rhubarb signal that winter is turning into spring—a happy message to convey at breakfast.

- 4 cups diced rhubarb
- ½ cup sugar
- 1 stick (2 to 3 in.) cinnamon
- 3 whole cloves
- ⅛ teaspoon ground nutmeg
- ¼ cup cold water

1. In a heavy 2-quart saucepan combine all ingredients. Bring to a boil, cover, reduce heat, and simmer until mixture has a saucelike consistency (8 to 10 minutes).

2. Pour into a bowl and let stand at room temperature until cool. Discard cinnamon stick and cloves. Serve at room temperature or chilled.

Serves 4.

MAPLE APPLE CRISP

Celebrate a fine fall day with bowls of this crumb-topped apple pudding.

- ½ cup each maple sugar and firmly packed brown sugar or 1 cup brown sugar
- ½ cup flour
- ¼ teaspoon each ground cinnamon and nutmeg
- ¼ cup cold butter or margarine
- 6 medium-sized tart cooking apples Whipping cream or half-and-half

1. Preheat oven to 350° F. Mix maple and brown sugar, flour, cinnamon, and nutmeg. Cut in butter until mixture is crumbly.

2. Peel, core, and slice apples (about 5 cups); spread in a buttered 8- or 9-inch square baking dish. Sprinkle sugar mixture evenly over apples, patting it together lightly.

3. Bake, uncovered, until topping is crisp and well browned and apples are tender (40 to 45 minutes). Serve warm with cream.

Serves 6.

Italian Baked Apples With Prunes (page 34) can be assembled the night before for a special treat first thing in the morning.

1. Preheat oven to 375° F. Core apples and remove about 1½ inches of peel around the stem end. Arrange in a buttered shallow baking dish just large enough to hold all the apples.

2. In a small bowl mix nuts, brown sugar, butter, and lemon rind. Divide mixture among cavities in apples. Add water to the dish to a depth of about ¼ inch.

3. Bake apples, uncovered, basting occasionally with liquid from bottom of dish, until tender when pierced with a fork (40 to 45 minutes).

4. Serve hot or at room temperature.

Serves 6.

ITALIAN BAKED APPLES WITH PRUNES

If you wish to serve these apples first thing in the morning, you can assemble the dish in its covered casserole the night before and refrigerate it. Then pop it into the oven as soon as you arise.

> 4 small tart cooking apples
> 1 cup dried prunes
> ½ teaspoon grated lemon rind
> 1 teaspoon vanilla extract
> 1 tablespoon lemon juice
> ¼ cup water
> ¼ teaspoon ground nutmeg
> ⅓ cup sugar

1. Preheat oven to 350° F. Core apples (do not peel) and place in a covered casserole just large enough to hold them. Arrange prunes around apples. Sprinkle with lemon rind, vanilla, lemon juice, and water. Mix nutmeg and sugar, and sprinkle evenly over fruits.

2. Cover and bake until apples and prunes are very tender (45 to 55 minutes).

3. Spoon an apple into each of 4 small soup or cereal bowls; break apples open with a spoon, and spoon prunes and juices over. Serve at once.

Serves 4.

Tart fall apples, sautéed in butter with lemon and nutmeg, make up Chunky Sautéed Apples With Lemon (page 32). Serve it hot with milk and freshly baked gingerbread for a memorable family breakfast. For a brunch dessert, flavor the apples with a splash of pear brandy.

NUTTY BAKED APPLES

Rome Beauty or McIntosh apples are good for baking and are delicious stuffed with chopped nuts, brown sugar, and butter.

> 6 large baking apples
> ⅓ cup finely chopped walnuts, pecans, or blanched almonds
> ⅓ cup firmly packed brown sugar
> 2 teaspoons butter or margarine, softened
> 1 teaspoon grated lemon rind

BREAKFAST STRAWBERRY SHORTCAKE

Homemade biscuits, buttered while they are hot, make this midwestern traditional shortcake distinctive. Although most would consider it a dessert, this shortcake is also irresistible for breakfast.

    4 cups strawberries (2 baskets)
    ½ cup sugar
    2 cups flour
    1 tablespoon baking powder
    ½ teaspoon salt
    ½ cup cold butter or margarine
    1 egg
    ⅓ cup half-and-half
       Half-and-half, for brushing
       Butter or margarine
       (optional)
       Whipped cream
       Vanilla Sugar (see page 30)

1. Hull strawberries and cut about 2 cups of them in halves; place halved berries in a bowl, mix lightly with ¼ cup of the sugar, and let stand at room temperature for about 1 hour. Set whole berries aside.

2. Preheat oven to 425° F. In a mixing bowl stir together remaining ¼ cup sugar, flour, baking powder, and salt. Cut in ½ cup butter to form coarse crumbs.

3. Beat egg with the ⅓ cup half-and-half. Add egg mixture, all at once, to flour mixture; mix gently just until a soft dough forms. Turn dough out onto a floured board or pastry cloth, turning to coat lightly with flour. Knead lightly just until dough is smooth. Pat or roll out about ¾ inch thick. Cut into 2½- to 3-inch rounds. Place on an ungreased baking sheet. Brush tops lightly with half-and-half.

4. Bake biscuits until golden (12 to 15 minutes).

5. To serve shortcakes, split hot biscuits, and spread cut surfaces lightly with butter, if desired. Place in shallow individual bowls and fill with sugared berries. Top with whipped cream and whole strawberries. Add Vanilla Sugar to taste.

Serves 6 to 8.

Treat yourself to a summer breakfast surprise—fresh Breakfast Strawberry Shortcake with hot, buttery biscuits. Although usually thought of as a dessert, it has most of the nutrients you need to start the day.

1. Combine egg yolks and sugar in top of a double boiler (off heat); beat until thick and pale. Mix in Marsala and place over simmering water. Cook, stirring constantly with a wire whisk, until thick (10 to 12 minutes).

2. Transfer egg yolk mixture to a large bowl, cover, and refrigerate until ready to serve.

3. Meanwhile, rinse berries carefully. Hull strawberries, reserving a few with leaves for garnish, if you wish. Pat berries dry.

4. Whip cream until stiff; carefully fold into egg yolk mixture until blended. Fold in berries. Serve in glasses, garnishing with whole berries, if you wish.

Serves 4 to 6.

BLACKBERRY COBBLER

When berries are in season, bake this luscious cobbler to serve for a summer breakfast on the back porch. It can be made in a large baking dish or in 4 individual ones.

      3 to 4 cups fresh blackberries,
         boysenberries, or
         olallieberries
    ⅔ cup sugar
      1 tablespoon lemon juice
    ¼ cup butter or margarine,
         softened
    ½ teaspoon vanilla extract
    ⅔ cup flour
      1 teaspoon baking powder
    ¼ teaspoon salt
    ⅛ teaspoon each *ground cinna-
         mon and nutmeg*
    ½ cup milk
         Whipping cream (optional)

1. Preheat oven to 400° F. Spread berries in a buttered, shallow 2-quart baking dish; sprinkle evenly with ⅓ cup of the sugar and lemon juice. (Or divide berries, sugar, and lemon juice among 4 buttered individual 2-cup baking dishes about 2 inches deep.)

Bubbling with fruit, Black-berry Cobbler, with its cakelike topping, makes a wonderful hot breakfast dish. Pour cream over each serving to cool and enrich the berries.

BERRIES ROMANOFF

Here is an elegant conclusion for a stylish brunch—strawberries and raspberries in a silken sherried cream. The beaten egg yolk mixture for the sauce can be cooked ahead and refrigerated before serving.

      3 egg yolks
    ⅔ cup sugar
    ⅔ cup dry Marsala or cream
         sherry
      3 cups strawberries (1½
         baskets)
      1 cup raspberries
    ⅔ cup whipping cream

36

2. Cream butter and remaining ⅓ cup sugar until fluffy. Beat in vanilla. Mix flour with baking powder, salt, cinnamon, and nutmeg. Add flour mixture to creamed mixture alternately with milk, beating until smooth after each addition. Spread over berries.

3. Bake until topping is well browned and springs back when center is touched lightly (35 to 40 minutes).

4. Serve warm or at room temperature, spooned into shallow bowls. Pour on cream, if desired.

Serves 4 to 6.

BANANAS FOSTER

A dramatic presentation characterizes this dish, which originated in New Orleans. Serve the flaming bananas over ice cream that has been scooped into individual dishes ahead of time and held in the freezer.

   ¼ cup butter or margarine
   ⅓ cup firmly packed brown
       sugar
   4 firm-ripe bananas
   ¼ teaspoon ground cinnamon
   ⅓ cup banana-flavored liqueur
   ½ cup rum
       Rich vanilla ice cream

1. In a chafing dish over an alcohol flame or in a cook-and-serve frying pan, melt butter over medium heat. Stir in brown sugar; cook and stir until sugar melts and bubbles.

2. Peel bananas and cut them in halves lengthwise, then crosswise, making 4 pieces from each. Add to butter mixture; sprinkle evenly with cinnamon. Carefully turn bananas, spooning sugar mixture over them. Lightly mix in banana-flavored liqueur.

3. Warm rum very slightly in a small metal pan; add to banana mixture, ignite, stir for a few minutes, then spoon flaming bananas around ice cream in individual dishes.

Serves 4.

FALL FAMILY BREAKFAST

Freshly Squeezed Orange Juice

Puffy Apple Fritters

Grilled Pork Sausages (see page 67)

Coffee or Milk

Choose your favorite tart apples for these crisply coated fritters. The batter contains beer, which makes it light and crisp when fried and adds a faintly malty flavor. The apple slices can be fried as long as an hour or two before serving, then reheated in the oven. Sift confectioners' sugar and a hint of cinnamon over them at the table.

PUFFY APPLE FRITTERS

   1 cup flour
   1 cup beer
   4 large apples, peeled and cored
       Flour
       Vegetable oil, for deep-frying
       Confectioners' sugar
       Ground cinnamon

1. In blender or food processor combine the 1 cup flour and beer. Whirl or process until smooth and well combined, stopping motor and scraping down sides of container with a rubber spatula once or twice to be sure all flour is incorporated. Pour batter into a shallow bowl.

2. Slice apples crosswise, about ½ inch thick. Dust slices lightly with flour.

3. Pour oil to a depth of at least 2 inches into a large, deep, heavy pan. Heat oil to 375° F. Dip apple rings into batter, coating thoroughly. Fry in heated oil, about 4 at a time, turning once, until golden brown on both sides (2 to 3 minutes).

4. Remove apple fritters with a slotted spoon, drain quickly on paper towels, then sprinkle generously with confectioners' sugar and a pinch of cinnamon, and serve hot.

Serves 4 to 6.

Note If made ahead, arrange fritters on several layers of fresh paper towels on baking sheets. Reheat in 350° F oven for 8 to 10 minutes.

Whether brown or white, farm-fresh or storebought, eggs offer infinite opportunities for breakfast and brunch variety.

Eggs

Can there be any single breakfast food more versatile than the egg? You can cook it in and eat it from its own little package. You can sizzle it in butter or poach it in liquid. To serve a crowd you can scramble a dozen at a time, and for showmanship, there are fluffy omelets and lofty soufflés. Each style of egg cookery has its own requirements. One useful rule is that eggs benefit from low-temperature cooking—too much heat toughens an egg, particularly the white, making it rubbery.

A soft-cooked egg from an eggcup is a child's delight. Serve it with cocoa, an orange, and Maple-Nut Bran Muffins (recipe on page 114).

EGGS COOKED IN THE SHELL

Whether soft or hard-cooked, eggs will taste best if you adjust the heat so that the water in which they cook never quite boils. Ideally, you should see tiny bubbles form on the bottom of the pan and rise slowly to the surface without breaking it.

SOFT-COOKED EGGS

1. Fill a saucepan with just enough water to cover the number of eggs to be cooked. Bring to a simmer and carefully lower eggs into the water. Simmer, uncovered, for 3 to 5 minutes, until eggs are done to taste.

2. Serve each egg, in shell, in an eggcup, cracking top lightly with a spoon and peeling about ½ inch of shell so egg can be eaten from remainder of shell. Or quickly cut egg in half, then use a spoon to scoop egg out into a small, warm dish.

HARD-COOKED EGGS

1. Place eggs in a single layer in a saucepan and cover with cold water. Bring to a boil over high heat; then reduce heat so bubbles rise slowly to the surface but do not break it. For tenderness and best color, the cooking water should *never boil* fully. Simmer, uncovered, for 20 minutes.

2. Pour off hot water, cover eggs with cold water, and let stand, changing cold water occasionally, until eggs are cool (about 30 minutes).

SHRIMP-CROWNED EGGS

A simple soft-cooked egg becomes quite another story when you top it with buttery little shrimp to stir into each spoonful. Another topping you might present in the same way is a teaspoon of caviar and a dollop of sour cream seasoned with chives.

2 teaspoons butter or margarine
1 green onion, finely chopped
¼ cup tiny peeled, cooked shrimp
6 eggs
    Hot buttered toast strips

1. Melt butter in a small frying pan over medium heat. Mix in onion and stir just until limp. Add shrimp and mix lightly, just until shrimp are heated through. Remove from heat and keep warm.

2. Soft-cook eggs according to directions on this page. Place eggs in eggcups and carefully slice off top fourth of each egg, using a serrated knife or egg scissors.

3. Scoop out and discard white from egg tops. Fill each eggshell with about 2 teaspoons of the shrimp mixture. Quickly invert shrimp-filled top onto the eggs and serve at once, accompanied by toast strips to dip into egg yolks.

Serves 6.

EGGS AND BROCCOLI CASSEROLE WITH HAM PINWHEEL BISCUITS

Accompany this colorful brunch main dish with a salad of crisp romaine lettuce and orange sections.

1 bunch (1¼ to 1½ lbs) broccoli
2 tablespoons butter or margarine
1½ tablespoons flour
¼ teaspoon salt
    Pinch each *white pepper and ground nutmeg*
1 cup milk
¾ cup diced sharp Cheddar cheese (¼-in. cubes)
4 hard-cooked eggs (at left), sliced

Ham Pinwheel Biscuits

1½ cups flour
2 teaspoons baking powder
½ teaspoon salt
⅓ cup cold butter or margarine
⅔ cup milk
1 tablespoon Dijon mustard
4 thin slices boiled ham

1. Preheat oven to 425° F. Cut off broccoli flowerets and separate into bite-sized pieces. Trim and discard ends of stems; peel lower portion of stems. Slice stems crosswise about ¼ inch thick.

2. Cook flowerets and stems in a small amount of boiling salted water (or steam on a rack) until barely crisp-tender (4 to 6 minutes). Place in a colander; rinse well with cold water to cool broccoli. Drain well and set aside.

3. In a medium saucepan heat butter over moderate heat until bubbly. Blend in flour, salt, pepper, and nutmeg. Remove from heat and gradually blend in milk. Cook, stirring constantly, until thickened; remove sauce from heat. Lightly fold in broccoli, cheese, and eggs.

4. Spread broccoli mixture in a buttered 2-quart casserole. Place Ham Pinwheel Biscuits, cut sides down, around edge of casserole with one in center.

5. Bake casserole until biscuits are well browned and sauce is bubbly (25 to 30 minutes). Serve at once, lifting biscuits onto plates, then spooning broccoli mixture beside them.

Serves 4 to 6.

Ham Pinwheel Biscuits

1. In a medium bowl mix flour, baking powder, and salt. Cut in butter until mixture is crumbly. Lightly mix in milk to make a soft dough. Turn dough out on a lightly floured board or pastry cloth and knead gently just until dough holds together (about 30 seconds). Roll out to an 8- by 10-inch rectangle. Spread mustard evenly over dough, not quite to edges. Cover mustard-spread area with slices of boiled ham, overlapping them slightly if necessary.

2. Starting with an 8-inch edge, roll dough up jelly-roll fashion. Moisten edge and pinch to seal. Cut into 8 equal slices.

NIPPY EGG AND CHEESE BUNS

A hard-cooked egg alone, peeled and eaten out-of-hand, makes a minimal breakfast in a pinch. Better still, however, is an English muffin broiled with this combination of hard-cooked eggs, olives, and Cheddar cheese. To save time, you can make the filling ahead, then spread and broil the muffins in the morning.

2 cups grated sharp Cheddar cheese
1 can (4½ oz) chopped ripe olives, well drained
Half a sweet red or green bell pepper, seeded and finely chopped
4 green onions, thinly sliced
2 hard-cooked eggs (see page 41), chopped
2 tablespoons catsup
2 teaspoons prepared mustard
4 whole wheat English muffins, split

1. Preheat broiler. Mix cheese, olives, red or green pepper, onions, eggs, catsup, and mustard until well combined.

2. Arrange English muffins on a baking sheet and broil until cut sides are slightly browned. Remove from oven and divide egg mixture evenly among the 8 muffin halves, spreading it to edges.

3. Broil, about 4 inches from heat, until cheese is melted and lightly browned (3 to 5 minutes).

Serves 4 (2 muffin halves each).

FRIED EGGS

To fry an egg, you can either baste it with the butter in which it cooks until the yolk is done to your taste, or cover it so that steam does the job.

BASIC FRIED EGGS

1. Using a frying pan just large enough to hold the number of eggs to be cooked, add about ½ tablespoon butter or margarine for each egg. Place pan over medium heat, swirling until butter melts and begins to sizzle.

2. Carefully break eggs into pan. Reduce heat to medium-low and cook, uncovered, occasionally spooning butter over eggs, until whites are set and a pale, translucent film covers yolks. *Or*, after adding eggs to pan and reducing heat, cover and cook until eggs are done to your liking as in first method.

FRIED EGGS WITH TOMATO SAUCE MEXICANA

Served on hot tortillas and blanketed with a chile-spiked tomato sauce, these spirited eggs are known in Mexico as *huevos rancheros*. The sauce can be made ahead, then reheated, to simplify last-minute preparation. Accompany with refried beans and hot buttered tortillas.

1 medium onion, chopped
1 tablespoon each *butter or margarine and olive oil*
1 clove garlic, minced or pressed
1 small, dried, hot red chile, crushed or 1 canned green chile, seeded and chopped
1 can (1 lb) tomatoes
1 teaspoon chili powder
½ teaspoon salt
¼ teaspoon sugar
8 corn tortillas
Oil for frying
8 eggs
¼ cup grated Monterey jack or mild Cheddar cheese
Sprigs of cilantro and sliced avocado, for garnish

Refried Beans

1 small onion, finely chopped
1 tablespoon each *butter or margarine and olive oil*
1 small clove garlic, minced or pressed
1 can (8¼ oz) refried beans
¼ teaspoon chili powder
⅓ cup grated Monterey jack or mild Cheddar cheese

1. In a medium frying pan cook onion in mixture of butter and olive oil over moderate heat until soft but not browned. Mix in garlic, red or green chile, tomatoes and their liquid (break up tomatoes with a fork), chili powder, salt, and sugar. Bring to a boil, cover, reduce heat, and simmer until sauce is reduced to about 1¾ cups, about 30 minutes longer. Keep warm; or make ahead, refrigerate, and then reheat.

2. Preheat oven to 250° F. Fry tortillas in about ½ inch of hot oil in large frying pan until limp or, if you prefer, until crisp and lightly browned. Drain on paper towels and keep warm in oven.

3. Pour out most of the oil, then fry eggs in the same pan (follow the recipe at left) until done to your liking.

4. For each serving, arrange 2 prepared tortillas on a large, warm plate. Top each with an egg, then spoon on hot tomato sauce and sprinkle with cheese. Garnish with cilantro and avocado.

Serves 4 (2 eggs each).

Refried Beans In a medium frying pan, cook onion in butter and olive oil, stirring until tender and lightly browned. Mix in garlic, refried beans, and chili powder. Cook over medium heat, stirring occasionally, until beans are heated through (3 to 5 minutes). Mix in cheese until melted.

Serves 4.

*Huevos rancheros—Fried Eggs
With Tomato Sauce Mexicana—
is the traditional breakfast
for vaqueros, or cowboys,
at south-of-the-border ranches.*

FRIED EGG MUFFIN SANDWICHES

One might describe this dish, borrowed from a popular fast-food concept, as no-fuss eggs Benedict. You just pick it up in both hands and eat it as a sandwich.

Try different combinations of types of ham and cheese for variety: baked ham with Cheddar cheese; boiled ham with Swiss cheese; coppa or prosciutto with provolone or Fontina cheese; Black Forest ham with Muenster cheese.

> 2 English muffins, split
> 3 tablespoons butter or
>   margarine
> 2 eggs
> 2 thin slices ham, cut to fit
>   muffins approximately
> 2 thin slices cheese

1. Toast muffins and keep warm.

2. To a large frying pan add butter and swirl over medium heat until butter melts and begins to sizzle. Carefully break eggs into pan. (Use egg poaching rings—see right—if you wish, to be sure egg has same shape as muffin; remove them after whites are set.) Add ham slices beside eggs. Reduce heat to medium-low, and cook, uncovered, occasionally spooning butter over eggs, until whites are set and a translucent film covers yolks. Turn ham slices once.

3. Place a cheese slice carefully on top of each egg.

4. To assemble each sandwich, place a ham slice on bottom half of muffin, top with egg and cheese, then cover with top half of muffin. Serve hot.

Serves 2.

CHEESE-SPECKLED EGGS

For a change of pace, sprinkle fried eggs with cheese and bacon bits shortly before they finish cooking.

> 2 tablespoons butter or
>   margarine
> 4 eggs
> ¼ cup grated sharp Cheddar
>   or provolone cheese
> 1 tablespoon each bacon bits
>   and finely chopped parsley

1. Melt butter in a medium frying pan over moderate heat, swirling until butter melts and begins to sizzle. Carefully break eggs into pan. Reduce heat to medium-low, cover, and cook for 1 minute.

2. Sprinkle evenly with cheese and bacon, cover again, and continue cooking until eggs are cooked to your liking (1½ to 2 minutes).

3. Serve sprinkled with parsley.

Serves 2 or 4.

POACHED EGGS

Elaborate poached egg dishes become much easier to manage when you learn a simple trick: The eggs can be poached hours ahead, even the night before, and refrigerated in a bowl of ice water. Shortly before you are ready to serve the eggs, warm them in a bowl of hot water.

BASIC POACHED EGGS

1. Immerse eggs (in shells) in rapidly boiling water for 5 seconds; remove eggs and set them aside. Pour water into a large, deep pan to a depth of about 2½ inches; place over high heat until water begins to boil. Then adjust heat so that water barely bubbles. Break eggs directly into water and cook gently until whites are firm (about 3 minutes).

2. Remove poached eggs from cooking water with a slotted spoon and serve at once, or immerse them in a bowl of ice water. Cover and refrigerate for several hours or overnight.

3. To reheat eggs, transfer to a bowl of water that is just hot to the touch and let stand 5 to 10 minutes.

POACHED EGGS WITH SORREL

Sorrel, a delightfully tart green, makes a flavorsome bed for poached eggs served with a creamy cheese sauce. If sorrel is not available, fresh spinach may be substituted, although it won't contribute quite such a distinctive taste.

> 8 eggs
> 1 shallot, finely chopped, or
>   2 tablespoons finely
>   chopped mild onion
> 3 tablespoons butter or
>   margarine
> 6 cups lightly packed sorrel
>   or spinach leaves (stems
>   removed), slivered
>   Pinch each salt, white pepper,
>   and ground nutmeg
>   Paprika and snipped chives,
>   for garnish

Sherried Swiss Cheese Sauce

      2   tablespoons butter or
            margarine
    1½   tablespoons flour
            Pinch each ground white
            pepper, ground nutmeg, and
            cayenne pepper
      1   cup half-and-half
      1   cup grated Swiss cheese
      ¼   cup dry sherry

1. Poach eggs according to directions on opposite page.

2. Prepare Sherried Swiss Cheese Sauce; keep warm (or reheat if made ahead and refrigerated), covered, in a double boiler over simmering water.

3. Reheat eggs if poached ahead (see step 3, opposite page).

4. In a large frying pan cook shallot in butter over medium heat until soft and lightly browned. Stir in sorrel and cook just until it is wilted. Season with salt, white pepper, and nutmeg. Divide mixture evenly into 4 warm, shallow individual casseroles.

5. Top each serving with 2 warm poached eggs. Spoon hot Sherried Swiss Cheese Sauce over eggs. Garnish with paprika and chives.

Serves 4.

Sherried Swiss Cheese Sauce

Melt butter in a 1½-quart saucepan. Stir in flour, white pepper, nutmeg, and cayenne; cook until bubbly. Remove from heat and gradually mix in half-and-half. Return to heat and cook, stirring, until thickened and bubbly. Stir in cheese until melted, then mix in sherry. Cover and refrigerate if made ahead.

Makes about 1⅔ cups.

POACHED EGGS WITH CHICKEN LIVERS

Raspberry wine vinegar, a favored seasoning of nouvelle cuisine enthusiasts, enhances the flavor of buttery chicken livers—a delicious foil for poached eggs on toast.

Accompany this brunch dish with creamed spinach or asparagus spears.

      6   eggs
      6   tablespoons butter or
            margarine
      6   slices firm white bread, crusts
            trimmed
      1   pound chicken livers, cut in
            halves
      2   shallots, finely chopped, or ¼
            cup finely chopped mild onion
      ½   teaspoon salt
            Freshly ground white or black
            pepper
      2   tablespoons raspberry wine
            vinegar or tarragon white
            wine vinegar
            Chopped parsley, for garnish

1. Poach eggs according to directions on opposite page, and refrigerate until ready to reheat.

2. Melt 3 tablespoons of the butter in a large frying pan over medium-low heat, add bread, and cook, turning once, until slices are crusty and well browned on both sides. Remove to warm plates and keep warm.

3. Reheat poached eggs as directed (see step 3, opposite page).

4. To pan in which bread was browned, add remaining 3 tablespoons butter and increase heat to medium-high. Add chicken livers and shallots and cook, turning livers carefully, until well browned on all sides. As livers brown, remove them from pan. (They should remain moist and pink in centers.) Sprinkle with salt and add pepper to taste. When all livers are removed from pan, add vinegar to pan and cook, stirring, to dissolve pan drippings. Remove from heat, return livers to pan, and stir lightly to coat with drippings. Keep liver mixture warm.

5. Place a warm egg on each toast slice. Spoon chicken livers and their liquid around eggs. Sprinkle with parsley. Serve at once.

Serves 6.

HELP FOR POACHING EGGS

Perfectly shaped poached eggs—cooked in the classic manner, in simmering water—can be difficult to achieve, especially if you are trying them for the first time. But help is available if you seek it out.

From England come deep, round rings; or from France, egg-shaped perforated stands. Either gives a poached egg a regular shape and prevents most of the white from drifting away from the yolk as the egg cooks.

To use either shape, first butter it well or spray it with a vegetable oil nonstick coating. Place it in the pan with the simmering water, break the egg into the form, then cook as directed on this page.

The rings can also be used for frying eggs—handy if you want them exactly round to match an English muffin.

In the absence of either of these forms, you might also use rings from wide-mouth canning jars (although, because they are grooved, they are more likely to stick to the eggs).

From the first sip of white wine to the last crumb of Chocolate-Almond Cookie Bark, you'll delight up to eight guests with this elegant Eggs Benedict Brunch.

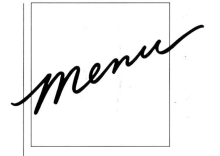

EGGS BENEDICT BRUNCH FOR EIGHT

Hazel's Ramos Gin Fizz

Eggs Benedict

Steamed Broccoli or Asparagus Spears

Bite-Sized Fruits

Chocolate-Almond Cookie Bark

White Wine

Coffee

Creamy gin fizzes (for eight people make two batches of the recipe on page 23) should please your guests while you assemble the elegant egg dish. It is really not difficult to manage when you have poached the eggs in advance— several hours or a day ahead.

Depending on the season, broccoli or asparagus can share the delicious Hollandaise Sauce with the eggs. The sauce can also be made well before your brunch.

EGGS BENEDICT

  16 eggs
   1 pound Canadian bacon or English muffin-sized ham, cut in 16 slices
   4 to 6 tablespoons butter or margarine
   8 English muffins, split

Hollandaise Sauce

   1 cup butter or margarine
   3 eggs
   3 tablespoons lemon juice
   1 teaspoon Dijon mustard
      Pinch cayenne pepper

1. Poach eggs according to directions on page 44, and refrigerate until ready to reheat.

2. Prepare Hollandaise Sauce and keep it warm over hot (*not* boiling) water in a double boiler.

3. In a large frying pan over moderate heat cook Canadian bacon in a little of the butter, adding more butter as needed (1 tablespoon at a time), until meat is lightly browned on both sides. Keep warm.

4. Reheat poached eggs as directed on page 44.

5. Broil split English muffins until crisp and golden brown.

6. For each serving, place 2 muffin halves on a warm plate and cover each with (in order) Canadian bacon, poached egg, and Hollandaise Sauce. Serve at once.

Serves 8.

Hollandaise Sauce In a small pan over medium heat melt butter or margarine until hot and foamy. While butter is melting, in blender or food processor place eggs, lemon juice, mustard, and cayenne. Turn blender or food processor on and begin pouring in hot butter in a slow, steady stream; whirl or process until all butter is added and sauce is smooth, frothy, and slightly thick. Serve warm.

Makes about 2 cups.

CHOCOLATE-ALMOND COOKIE BARK

  ¾ cup butter or margarine, softened
  ⅓ cup each granulated sugar and firmly packed light brown sugar
  2 tablespoons coffee-flavored liqueur
 1½ cups flour
  1 package (6 oz) semisweet chocolate chips
  ½ cup slivered almonds

1. Preheat oven to 375° F. In large bowl of electric mixer, cream butter and sugars, beating until light and fluffy. Gradually blend in liqueur.

2. Gradually add flour, mixing until blended. Stir in chocolate chips.

3. Spread mixture evenly in an ungreased, shallow 15- by 10-inch baking pan. Sprinkle evenly with almonds, pressing them lightly into dough.

4. Bake until cookies are well browned (18 to 20 minutes). Cool completely in pan on a wire rack, then turn out and break into irregular pieces.

Makes about 4 dozen cookies.

POACHED EGGS IN BAKED POTATOES

Based on an old French recipe for a country supper dish, these poached eggs also make a splendid brunch. Serve them with broccoli spears and follow with a dessert of fruit compote and ginger cookies.

- 4 large baking potatoes
- ¼ cup butter or margarine
- 4 eggs
- 2 to 3 tablespoons milk
- ¼ teaspoon salt
  Pinch each *white pepper and ground nutmeg*
- 1 cup (about ¼ lb) *julienned ham*
- ¼ cup each *soft bread crumbs and grated Parmesan cheese*

Mornay Sauce

- 1 tablespoon butter or margarine
- 1 tablespoon flour
- ⅛ teaspoon salt
  Pinch each *white pepper and nutmeg*
- 1 cup *half-and-half*
- 1 egg yolk
- ⅓ cup *grated Swiss cheese*

1. Preheat oven to 450° F. Scrub potatoes and pat dry; rub skins lightly with a little of the butter and pierce each in several places with a fork. Bake until tender when pierced, 50 minutes to 1 hour.

2. Poach eggs according to directions on page 44; refrigerate until needed.

3. Preheat oven to 450° F. When potatoes are cool enough to handle, cut a slice about ½ inch thick from the top of each, reserving slices. Carefully scoop out most of the inside of each potato; measure 1½ cups potato (reserve any remaining potato for other uses) into a mixing bowl.

Add 1 tablespoon of the remaining butter, 2 tablespoons of the milk, salt, white pepper, and nutmeg. Beat until fluffy, adding up to 1 tablespoon more milk to make a smooth (but not too soupy) mixture.

4. Return mashed potatoes to potato shells and use the back of a spoon to make an egg-shaped hollow in each.

5. In a medium frying pan, cook ham in 1 tablespoon more of the butter, stirring until crisp and lightly browned.

6. Into the hollow in each potato, place 1 tablespoon Mornay Sauce, a fourth of the ham, and a drained poached egg. Place potatoes on a baking sheet or in shallow individual casseroles and spoon remaining sauce evenly over eggs. Top each potato with a tablespoon *each* of bread crumbs and cheese. Melt remaining butter and drizzle evenly over tops of potatoes. Place slices cut from tops beside potatoes.

7. Bake until potatoes are heated through and topping browns lightly (10 to 15 minutes). Serve at once, with a top slice beside each potato.

Serves 4.

Mornay Sauce In a small saucepan over medium heat melt butter. Stir in flour, salt, white pepper, and nutmeg; cook until bubbling. Remove from heat and gradually mix in half-and-half; cook, stirring, until thick. In a small bowl beat egg yolk. Stir in a little of the heated sauce, then return mixture to pan. Cook over low heat, stirring constantly, until thick. Mix in cheese until melted, then remove from heat.

POACHED EGGS WITH LEEKS

A touch of caviar adds an elegant finish to these poached eggs.

- 8 eggs
- 3 large leeks
- 2 tablespoons butter or margarine
- ⅓ cup dry white wine
- ⅔ cup whipping cream
- 1 teaspoon each *lemon juice and Dijon mustard*
- ¼ teaspoon each *salt and white pepper*
- 1 tablespoon finely chopped parsley
- 2 tablespoons black or red caviar (or 1 tablespoon each)

1. Poach eggs according to directions on page 44, and refrigerate until ready to reheat.

2. Cut off root ends of leeks; remove coarse outer leaves. Cut off upper parts of green tops, leaving about 10-inch-long leeks. Split lengthwise, from stem ends, cutting to within about 1 inch of root ends. Soak in cold water for several minutes; then separate leaves under running water to rinse away any clinging grit; drain well. Slice about ⅛ inch thick.

3. In a large frying pan melt butter over medium heat. Add sliced leeks; cook, stirring often, until leeks are tender and bright green (6 to 8 minutes). Remove leeks and divide them among 4 individual shallow au gratin dishes; keep warm.

4. Reheat poached eggs as directed on page 44.

5. To pan in which leeks were cooked add wine, cream, lemon juice, mustard, and salt and white pepper. Bring mixture to a boil and cook, stirring, until thickened and reduced to about ½ cup. Remove from heat and mix in parsley.

6. Place 2 warm eggs on top of leeks in each dish; spoon cream sauce over and around them, dividing it evenly; then top each egg with a dollop of caviar. Serve at once.

Serves 4.

SCRAMBLED EGGS

When the cupboard is otherwise bare, you can always count on scrambled eggs for an enjoyable, quick, and nourishing breakfast or brunch. It's easy to add other ingredients to make the eggs more interesting, and even the least skilled beginner can learn the fundamentals of scrambling creamy, golden eggs.

Place the eggs in a bowl large enough to allow for brisk beating. Season with salt—about ¼ teaspoon for every 3 eggs (unless you plan to add other salty ingredients)—and a pinch of pepper. Add about 1 table-spoon of water, milk, or cream for every 3 eggs. Then beat with a fork, wire whisk, or egg beater until yolks and whites are completely blended.

As with other types of eggs, cook-ing scrambled eggs over moderate to low heat assures that they will be moist and tender. Heat butter or margarine in a frying pan, then add the egg mixture. As the eggs begin to set, *slowly* stir the mixture with a wooden spoon or spatula, lifting cooked portions and letting the un-cooked eggs flow underneath. Cook just until eggs are set, but still shiny and moist looking.

Other ingredients might be added to the butter in the same pan in which the eggs are to be scrambled. For example, cook onions, chopped green pepper, sliced mushrooms, or bits of ham first, then reduce heat before adding the eggs. Or sprinkle the eggs with your favorite grated cheese when they are nearly cooked. A scattering of snipped parsley or other fresh herbs at the finish also adds flavor.

ITALIAN EGG AND VEGETABLE SCRAMBLE

Potatoes, Italian sausage, onion, green pepper, and tomato make this a hearty, late-morning brunch dish.

- 2 tablespoons butter or margarine
- 1 tablespoon olive oil
- 1 medium potato, cut in ½-inch cubes
- ½ pound Italian sausages
- 1 small onion, thinly sliced and separated into rings
- ¼ cup finely chopped green bell pepper
- 8 eggs
- 2 tablespoons half-and-half
- ½ teaspoon salt
- ⅛ teaspoon dried oregano
- 1 firm-ripe tomato, seeded and chopped
  Hot buttered and toasted Italian or French bread
- ¼ cup grated Parmesan cheese
  Chopped parsley, for garnish

1. Heat butter and olive oil in a large frying pan. Add potato and begin cooking over medium heat, stirring occasionally. Meanwhile, remove sausage casings and crumble the meat. Add to frying pan, cooking and stirring until lightly browned. Add onion and green pepper, cooking and stirring occasionally until onions are limp and potatoes are done.

2. In a bowl, beat eggs with half-and-half, salt, and oregano until well combined. Add tomatoes and egg mixture, all at once, to vegetable mixture. Reduce heat to low and cook, stirring lightly as eggs begin to thicken, until eggs are creamy and softly set.

3. Spoon eggs over slices of hot buttered and toasted Italian bread, and sprinkle with cheese, then parsley.

Serves 4 to 6.

CALICO SCRAMBLED EGGS

Colorful red pepper and green onion dot these scrambled eggs.

- ½ cup finely chopped sweet red bell pepper
- 6 green onions, thinly sliced
- ¼ cup butter or margarine
- 8 eggs
- 2 tablespoons water or milk
- ½ teaspoon salt
  Pinch white pepper

1. Cook red pepper and green onions in butter in a large frying pan over medium heat, stirring occasionally, until vegetables are soft but not browned.

2. In a bowl beat eggs with water, salt, and white pepper until well combined. Add egg mixture, all at once, to vegetable mixture. Reduce heat to low and cook, stirring lightly as eggs begin to thicken, until eggs are creamy and softly set. Serve at once.

Serves 4.

Hot coffee, chilled tomato juice, and chive- and ham-sprinkled Scrambled Eggs in a Crisp Crust make a colorful and complete breakfast.

SCRAMBLED EGGS IN A CRISP CRUST

Serve fluffy scrambled eggs in a baked pastry for an unusual presentation. You can bake the crust ahead, then reheat it in the oven while preparing the eggs.

  8 eggs
  2 tablespoons water
  ½ teaspoon salt
     Pinch each *ground nutmeg and white pepper*
  ¼ *pound thinly sliced Westphalian ham or prosciutto, julienned*
  6 tablespoons butter or margarine
     Snipped chives or chopped parsley, for garnish

Crisp Wheat Pastry

  ¾ cup all-purpose flour
  ⅔ cup graham or whole wheat flour
  ½ teaspoon salt
  ⅛ teaspoon sugar
  ¼ cup cold butter or margarine
  2 tablespoons lard
  2 tablespoons grated Parmesan cheese
  1 teaspoon lemon juice
  1 to 1½ tablespoons cold water

1. Prepare pastry as directed, bake, and keep warm; if baked ahead, reheat in a 350° F oven until heated through (6 to 8 minutes).

2. In a large bowl beat eggs with water, salt, nutmeg, and white pepper until well combined.

3. In a small frying pan cook ham strips in 2 tablespoons of the butter until lightly browned; keep warm.

4. Melt 3 tablespoons of the remaining butter in a large frying pan over low heat. Add egg mixture all at once. Cook, stirring lightly as eggs begin to thicken, until eggs are creamy. Cut remaining 1 tablespoon butter into bits and add to eggs, stirring until softly set.

5. Spoon scrambled eggs into hot pastry. Scatter ham strips evenly over eggs, sprinkle lightly with chives, and serve at once.

Serves 4 to 6.

Crisp Wheat Pastry

1. Preheat oven to 450° F. Mix flours, salt, and sugar. Cut in butter, lard, and cheese until crumbly. Gradually mix in lemon juice and cold water until mixture clings together.

2. Press dough into a flattened ball. Roll out on a floured board or pastry cloth to fit a 9-inch pie pan. Fit into pie pan; trim and flute edge. Pierce all over with a fork to prevent pastry from bubbling. Bake until lightly browned (10 to 12 minutes).

OMELETS AND FRITTATAS

If scrambled eggs enjoy an anyone-can-do-it reputation, the omelet, by contrast, is often thought by novice cooks to be somewhat intimidating. Perhaps it does require a bit of practice to turn an omelet out smoothly. But once the knack is learned, making an omelet can be the quickest and most delicious route to a great breakfast.

One of the nicest things about omelets is that they can be filled with virtually anything you have in the refrigerator—cheese, sautéed vegetables, or bits of meat or seafood. Mastering the art of making fine omelets can earn you the reputation of being a great cook. All it takes is eggs and a few odds and ends (even leftovers), artfully combined.

Although you might make a single 4- to 6-egg omelet and divide it in half to serve two, for three or more people the most practical route is to cook individual omelets. Prepare fillings, keeping them warm if necessary. Beat eggs with seasonings in a large bowl. Have butter at hand.

Then, using one or more omelet pans, cook and fill an omelet for each person. Omelet-making is so quick that one cook can serve several people in just a few minutes. If you are entertaining guests who enjoy cooking, why not let each person turn out his or her own omelet.

BASIC OMELETS

> *9 eggs*
> *3 tablespoons water*
> *½ teaspoon salt*
> *Pinch each ground nutmeg and white pepper*
> *3 to 4 tablespoons butter or margarine*

1. In a large bowl beat eggs with water, salt, nutmeg, and white pepper until well blended (about 30 seconds).

2. For each omelet heat about 1 tablespoon of the butter in an 8-inch omelet pan over medium-high heat until it begins to foam. Pour in a third to a fourth of the egg mixture.

3. At first, slide pan back and forth to keep omelet from sticking. As the bottom begins to set, slip a thin spatula under eggs, tilting pan and lifting cooked portion to let uncooked egg mixture flow under it to the center. Repeat until most of the omelet is set, but center and top are still moist and creamy.

4. For a filled omelet, spoon filling across center in line with handle. Have a warm serving plate ready. Loosen one side of the omelet with spatula and fold it about a third over the remainder. Then hold pan over serving plate so the other side begins to slide out. Flip omelet so that previously folded side folds over, producing an omelet folded into thirds with center third on top.

Makes 3 or 4 individual omelets.

A quick, French-style, folded omelet is the heart of many a breakfast or brunch. Almost anything is delicious inside: fresh vegetables, fruits, cheese, seafood, or meats. See the tips on page 53 for special instructions on cooking and folding these egg-based favorites.

BRIE AND HAM OMELET

The warmth of a just-cooked omelet melts room-temperature Brie cheese so that its distinctive flavor spreads throughout; you won't need much of the cheese to fill several omelets. Accompany this brunch dish with a watercress and mushroom salad and a light red wine.

- ¼ pound Brie cheese
- 6 tablespoons butter or margarine
- 2 tablespoons chopped shallots or mild onion
- ¼ pound thinly sliced baked ham or Black Forest ham, julienned
- 2 tablespoons chopped parsley
- ¼ teaspoon dried tarragon
  Basic Omelets (see page 51)

1. Let cheese stand at room temperature for about 1 hour to soften. Scoop cheese from rind, discarding rind, and set cheese aside.

2. In a medium frying pan over moderate heat, melt 2 tablespoons of the butter and cook shallots and ham, stirring occasionally until ham browns lightly and shallots are soft. Stir in parsley and tarragon. Keep warm while preparing omelets.

3. Prepare 3 or 4 Basic Omelets, following directions on page 51 and cooking them in remaining butter. Spoon dollops of cheese over each, using a third or a fourth of it. Then spoon a third or a fourth of the ham mixture over the cheese on top of each omelet.

4. Fold as directed and serve at once.
Serves 3 or 4.

SHRIMP AND AVOCADO OMELET

The filling for this omelet requires virtually no cooking—just warming through. The combination is delicious with sprouted wheat bread toast.

- 6 green onions, thinly sliced
- 6 tablespoons butter or margarine
- ¼ pound small peeled, cooked shrimp
- 1 teaspoon lemon juice
  Basic Omelets (see page 51)
- 1 medium avocado, peeled, seeded, and diced
- 3 to 4 tablespoons sour cream

1. In a medium frying pan over moderate heat, cook onions in 2 tablespoons of the butter until limp and bright green. Add shrimp and lemon juice, stirring just until shrimp are heated through. Keep warm.

2. Immediately prepare 3 or 4 Basic Omelets, following directions on page 51, and cooking them in remaining butter. Use a third or a fourth of the shrimp filling for each, then add a third or a fourth of the avocado and a dollop of sour cream.

3. Fold as directed and serve at once.
Serves 3 or 4.

FRESH SPINACH AND MUSHROOM OMELET

To complement the sprightly fresh green of the spinach that fills this omelet, add a garnish of tomato wedges and a fluff of alfalfa sprouts.

- ½ pound mushrooms, thinly sliced
- ¼ cup finely chopped red onion
- 3 tablespoons butter or margarine
- ¼ teaspoon each salt and grated lemon rind
- ⅛ teaspoon each dried tarragon and ground nutmeg
- 4 cups lightly packed fresh spinach leaves, washed, stems removed
  Basic Omelets (see page 51) -
- 1 small package (3 oz) cream cheese, cut in ½-inch cubes

1. Cook mushrooms and red onion in heated butter in a large frying pan over medium-high heat, stirring occasionally, until mushrooms are lightly browned. Mix in salt, lemon rind, tarragon, and nutmeg. Then add spinach, stirring over medium heat just until leaves are coated with mushroom mixture and beginning to wilt. Remove from heat.

2. Immediately prepare 3 or 4 Basic Omelets, following directions on page 51. Use a third or a fourth of the spinach and mushroom filling for each, dotting it with a third or a fourth of the cream cheese cubes.

3. Fold as directed and serve at once.
Serves 3 or 4.

CURRIED VEGETABLE OMELETS

Here is a meatless omelet with bold flavors. It is filled with toasted almonds and tender-crisp vegetables piquantly seasoned with curry powder. For breakfast or brunch add rye or whole wheat toast and freshly squeezed orange juice.

- 1 cup small broccoli flowerets
- ½ cup thinly sliced carrots
- 1 medium onion, slivered
- ¼ cup finely chopped sweet red bell pepper
- 2 tablespoons butter or margarine
- 1 tablespoon olive oil or salad oil
- ½ teaspoon mustard seeds, slightly crushed
- 1 teaspoon curry powder
- 1 clove garlic, minced or pressed
- ¼ teaspoon ground cumin
- ½ teaspoon each *salt and grated lemon rind*
  Basic Omelets (see page 51)
- 3 to 4 tablespoons toasted sliced almonds

1. Cook broccoli and carrots in a small amount of boiling salted water (or steam on a rack) until crisp-tender (4 to 6 minutes). Drain well and set aside.

2. In a medium frying pan, cook onion and red pepper in mixture of butter and oil with mustard seed and curry powder over medium heat, stirring frequently, until onion is soft but not brown. Mix in garlic, cumin, salt, lemon rind, and cooked vegetables. Keep warm.

3. Prepare 3 or 4 Basic Omelets, following directions on page 51. Use a third or a fourth of the curried vegetable filling for each, sprinkling each with about 1 tablespoon of the almonds.

Serves 3 or 4.

STRAWBERRY BLINTZ OMELETS

This delicate omelet is filled with fluffy cream cheese and brown sugar and covered with fresh strawberries and sliced almonds. Accompany it with hot breakfast tea and warm brioches or toasted bagels.

- 1 basket (about 2 cups) strawberries
- 2 tablespoons Vanilla Sugar (see page 30)
- 1 small package (3 oz) cream cheese, softened
- 1 tablespoon milk or half-and-half
  Pinch ground nutmeg
  Basic Omelets (see page 51 and step 3 below)
- 3 to 4 tablespoons light brown sugar
- 3 to 4 tablespoons toasted sliced almonds

1. Hull strawberries, reserving a few with leaves for garnish; cut hulled berries in halves. Place in a bowl, mix lightly with Vanilla Sugar, and let stand at room temperature while preparing filling and omelets.

2. In a small bowl beat cream cheese with milk and nutmeg until fluffy.

3. Prepare 3 or 4 Basic Omelets, omitting pepper from egg mixture and following directions on page 51. Use a third or a fourth of the cream cheese mixture and about 1 tablespoon of the brown sugar to fill each. Fold omelets as directed.

4. Serve omelets on warm plates, spooning strawberries over and sprinkling each with about 1 tablespoon almonds. Serve at once.

Serves 3 or 4.

HOW TO MAKE AN OMELET

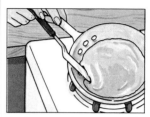

1. *As egg mixture sets, tilt pan and gently lift cooked portions with a spatula, enabling the uncooked egg to flow underneath.*

2. *When most of the omelet is set but top is still slightly moist, spoon filling across center in a line with the handle.*

3. *With warm serving plate in readiness, make first fold by loosening omelet and folding a third of it (from far side) toward the middle.*

4. *Tip pan with unfolded edge of omelet over plate, guiding with spatula, then flip quickly so previously folded edge turns over.*

While the Country Vegetable Frittata slowly cooks to golden perfection, sizzle sausages on a grill for a hearty brunch. See the Special Feature on page 67 for tips on making your own pork sausage.

COUNTRY VEGETABLE FRITTATA

Frittata is the Italian word for "omelet," but a frittata differs from our version of an omelet in several ways. A frittata can be made in a larger pan and cut in wedges to serve several people. Although omelets are usually served as soon as they are cooked, a frittata may be eaten hot, lukewarm, or even cold. It is usually turned out before it has completed cooking, inverted, and returned to the frying pan to brown on both sides. The filling for a frittata becomes part of the egg mixture. This one, which in Italian is called *frittata alla contadina*, contains zucchini, carrot, herbs, onion, and peas. You might serve it with grilled Italian sausages and a crusty loaf of whole wheat bread.

   1 medium zucchini
   1 medium carrot, thinly sliced
   8 eggs
   3 tablespoons water
  ¼ teaspoon salt
  Dash each pepper and
     ground nutmeg
   2 tablespoons grated
     Parmesan cheese
   2 tablespoons each butter or
     margarine and olive oil
  ¼ cup thinly slivered onion
   1 clove garlic, minced or pressed
  ¼ teaspoon dried oregano
   2 tablespoons chopped parsley
  ¼ cup thawed frozen peas

1. Cut zucchini into quarters, lengthwise; then cut crosswise into ¼-inch-thick slices. Cook carrots in a small amount of boiling salted water (or steam on a rack) until crisp-tender (4 to 6 minutes), adding zucchini for last 2 minutes of cooking time. Drain vegetables well and set aside.

2. Beat eggs in a large bowl with the 3 tablespoons water, salt, pepper, nutmeg, and cheese.

3. Melt butter with 1 tablespoon of the olive oil in a well-seasoned or nonstick 10- to 11-inch omelet pan over medium heat. Mix in onion and cook until limp. Add garlic, oregano, parsley, peas, and carrot mixture, stirring to coat with onions.

4. Pour egg mixture into pan and cook without stirring until about ¼ inch around the outer edge is set. With a wide spatula, lift some of the egg mixture from sides of pan, all the way around, tipping pan to let uncooked egg flow to pan bottom. Continue cooking until eggs are almost set but top of center is still moist and creamy.

5. Invert a large, round, flat plate (a little larger than the frying pan) over pan. Holding plate and pan together, turn frittata out onto plate. Add remaining 1 tablespoon olive oil to pan, swirl to coat pan, then slide frittata from plate back into frying pan. Cook for about 2 minutes more to brown bottom lightly, then invert frittata onto a serving plate. Cut in wedges to serve.

Serves 4.

BAKED ARTICHOKE AND ONION FRITTATA

This frittata needs little attention, because it is baked in a casserole rather than being cooked on top of the range. Add crusty rolls and an avocado salad to complete the brunch menu.

    1 package (9 oz) frozen
      artichoke hearts
    1 medium onion, slivered
    1 tablespoon each olive oil
      and butter or margarine
    ¼ teaspoon dried oregano
    1 small clove garlic, minced
      or pressed
    ¾ cup grated Parmesan cheese
    6 eggs
    ½ cup milk
    ¼ teaspoon salt
    ⅛ teaspoon each white pepper
      and ground nutmeg
    1 cup grated Monterey jack
      cheese

1. Preheat oven to 350° F. Cook artichoke hearts according to package directions until just tender; drain well.

2. In a medium frying pan, cook onion in mixture of olive oil and butter over moderate heat until soft and beginning to brown. Mix in oregano, garlic, and artichokes. Remove from heat.

3. Generously grease a shallow 1½- to 2-quart round or oval casserole or baking pan. Coat sides and bottom with ¼ cup of the Parmesan cheese. Spoon artichoke mixture evenly over bottom.

4. Beat together eggs, milk, salt, white pepper, and nutmeg. Mix in Monterey jack cheese and ¼ cup more of the Parmesan cheese. Pour over artichokes.

5. Bake, uncovered, for 30 minutes. Sprinkle evenly with remaining ¼ cup Parmesan cheese. Continue baking until frittata is puffed and golden brown (5 to 8 minutes).

Serves 4.

TOMATO FRITTATA

A homemade tomato sauce, accented by basil, colors and flavors this lively frittata. Try it with French bread and artichokes vinaigrette.

    1 small onion, finely chopped
    2 tablespoons olive oil
    1 clove garlic, minced or pressed
    1 can (1 lb) tomatoes
    1 teaspoon dried basil
    ½ teaspoon salt
    ⅛ teaspoon pepper
    6 eggs
    1 tablespoon finely chopped
      parsley
    3 tablespoons butter or
      margarine

1. Cook onion in olive oil in a medium frying pan until soft but not brown. Add garlic, tomatoes (coarsely chopped) and their liquid, basil, salt, and pepper. Bring to a boil, cover, reduce heat, and simmer for 10 minutes. Uncover and boil gently, stirring occasionally, until tomato mixture is thickened and reduced to about 1⅓ cups. Cool to room temperature.

2. Beat eggs in a large bowl; mix in tomato sauce and parsley. Melt 2 tablespoons of the butter in a 9-inch omelet pan over medium-low heat. Pour egg mixture into pan and cook, without stirring, until about ¼ inch around the outer edge is set. With a wide spatula, lift some of the egg mixture from sides of pan, all the way around, tipping pan to let un-cooked egg flow to pan bottom. Continue cooking until eggs are al-most set but top of center is still moist and creamy.

3. Invert a large, round, flat plate (a little larger than the frying pan) over pan. Holding pan and plate together, turn frittata out onto plate. Add re-maining 1 tablespoon butter to pan, swirl to melt butter, then slide frittata from plate back into frying pan. Cook for about 2 minutes more to brown bottom lightly. Invert frittata onto a serving plate. Cut in wedges.

Serves 4.

BAKED EGGS

Baked—or shirred—eggs are easy to prepare, yet seem elegant when served in individual baking dishes.

BAKED EGGS IN TOMATO SAUCE

Accompany these Italian-style baked eggs with warm Italian or French bread and patties of homemade sau-sage (see page 67), if you wish.

    1 large onion, thinly slivered
    ½ pound mushrooms, thinly
      sliced
    ¼ cup chopped green bell pepper
    ¼ cup olive oil
    1 clove garlic, minced or pressed
    1 can (1 lb) tomatoes
    ¼ cup dry white wine
    ⅓ cup finely chopped parsley
    ½ teaspoon each salt, ground
      cinnamon, and dried basil
    ¼ teaspoon each pepper and
      dried oregano
    6 eggs
    ½ cup grated Monterey jack
      cheese

1. Preheat oven to 325° F. In a large frying pan cook onion, mushrooms, and green pepper in heated olive oil over medium heat, stirring frequently, until onions are soft and mushrooms are lightly browned. Mix in garlic, tomatoes (coarsely chopped) and their liquid, wine, parsley, and sea-sonings. Bring to a boil, cover, re-duce heat, and simmer 10 minutes.

2. Uncover and boil gently, stirring occasionally, until tomato mixture is thickened and reduced to about 2½ cups. Transfer to a greased, shallow 2-quart casserole. With the back of a spoon make 6 egg-sized hollows. Break an egg into each.

3. Cover and bake for 12 minutes. Uncover, sprinkle with cheese, and continue baking until eggs are set to your liking and cheese melts (5 to 10 minutes).

Serves 6.

To flavor Parmesan Baked Eggs, you can add such toppings as green onions or chives, salsa, crumbled bacon, or grated cheese.

SWISS BAKED EGGS

Baked eggs with a fonduelike flavor make an appealing breakfast for six, with French bread toast and café au lait or hot chocolate.

¼ pound Swiss cheese, thinly sliced
1 green onion, thinly sliced
1 tablespoon chopped parsley
6 eggs
  Salt, ground nutmeg, and freshly ground pepper
¼ cup whipping cream
2 tablespoons dry white wine
  Hot, buttered, toasted French bread slices

1. Preheat oven to 325° F. Line sides and bottom of a generously buttered, shallow 1½-quart baking dish (about 8 inches by 11 to 12 inches) with cheese. Sprinkle evenly with onion and parsley. Break eggs carefully into dish and sprinkle lightly with salt, nutmeg, and pepper.

2. In a medium bowl beat cream with wine just until well blended; pour around and between eggs.

3. Bake, uncovered, until eggs are set to your liking (12 to 18 minutes). Place eggs on hot, buttered, toasted French bread slices. Stir any melted cheese and cream remaining in baking dish until smooth, then spoon over eggs and toast.

Serves 6.

PARMESAN BAKED EGGS

In the basic recipe, eggs are baked in buttered shallow casseroles with Parmesan cheese. For variety try Prosciutto Baked Eggs or the topping variations.

> 2 tablespoons butter or margarine
> ¼ cup grated Parmesan cheese
> 4 eggs
> Salt, ground nutmeg, and freshly ground pepper
> Chopped Italian (flat-leaf) parsley, for garnish

1. Preheat oven to 325° F. Using about half of the butter, grease 4 shallow individual baking dishes about 5 inches in diameter. Coat each with 1 tablespoon of the cheese.

2. Break an egg into each dish. Sprinkle lightly with salt, nutmeg, and pepper. Dot with remaining butter.

3. Bake, uncovered, until eggs are set to your liking (12 to 15 minutes). Sprinkle with Italian parsley before serving.

Serves 4.

Prosciutto Baked Eggs Do not coat baking dishes with Parmesan cheese. Instead, cook 4 thin slices prosciutto or other ham in butter or margarine until lightly browned, and line each baking dish with a prosciutto slice. Pour in any butter from frying pan. Continue as in basic recipe with eggs, salt, nutmeg, and pepper. Then sprinkle each egg with 1 tablespoon grated Parmesan cheese instead of dotting with butter.

Topping Variations After baking eggs, sprinkle with one or more of these toppings: thinly sliced green onions or snipped chives, red or green chile salsa, caviar, sour cream crumbled crisp bacon, or grated Swiss or sharp Cheddar cheese.

SOUFFLÉS

Soufflés share with omelets an aura of sophistication—and have the edge on omelets for degree of difficulty. But like omelets, once you have learned the basics, you can make any soufflé. A dramatically puffed soufflé is such a hit for a brunch entrée that it is well worth mastering the quite straightforward steps in creating one.

The basis for a soufflé is generally a fairly thick white sauce, to which may be added puréed or cooked vegetables or fruit, cheese or wine— or some of each. Egg yolks are blended into the sauce. Then it is leavened with beaten egg whites. It is their expansion as the soufflé bakes that makes it rise and billow.

The only tricky part of preparing a soufflé has to do with the egg whites. First, they must be beaten enough but not too much—just until small, slightly curved peaks form. Then they must be folded lightly and carefully into the sauce just until incorporated, using a rubber spatula and a circular, up-and-over motion. Stirring in or overfolding the egg whites may release so much air that the soufflé will fail to rise.

Next comes baking. Be sure the oven is preheated before putting the soufflé inside. Don't open the door until the soufflé is almost done. When it is ready, serve it *at once!* Sound advice for this delicate dish is to let your guests wait for the soufflé if need be, but never the other way around.

Timing the process is not as hard as you might think. You can make the sauce and blend in the egg yolks up to an hour or more before baking the soufflé. Just before baking, beat the egg whites and fold them in.

FOUR CHEESES SOUFFLÉ

An idea borrowed from the popular pasta sauce—combining four Italian-style cheeses—gives this soufflé a rich flavor. For brunch add a tomato salad with basil dressing and rolls.

> Butter or margarine
> 2 tablespoons grated Parmesan cheese
> 3 tablespoons butter or margarine
> 3 tablespoons flour
> Dash cayenne pepper
> ¼ teaspoon each *salt and dry mustard*
> ⅛ teaspoon ground nutmeg
> 1 cup milk
> ¼ cup each *crumbled Gorgonzola or other blue-vein cheese and diced Fontina cheese (¼-in. cubes)*
> ¾ cup grated Swiss cheese
> 5 eggs, separated

1. Preheat oven to 350° F. Generously butter a 1½-quart soufflé dish. Coat evenly with the Parmesan cheese.

2. In a large, heavy saucepan melt the 3 tablespoons butter over medium heat. Stir in flour, cayenne, salt, dry mustard, and nutmeg; cook, stirring, until bubbly.

3. Remove from heat and gradually blend in milk. Return to heat and cook, stirring constantly, until thickened. Add Gorgonzola and Fontina cheeses and ½ cup of the Swiss cheese; stir until cheese melts. Remove pan from heat and beat in egg yolks, one at a time.

4. Beat egg whites until they form short, distinct peaks. Fold about half the whites thoroughly into the sauce, then gently fold in remaining whites. Pour into prepared soufflé dish. With the tip of a spatula, draw a circle around circumference of the soufflé about 1 inch in from side of dish. Top with rest of Swiss cheese.

5. Bake until soufflé is well browned and crust feels firm when tapped lightly (35 to 40 minutes).

Serves 4.

SPINACH SOUFFLÉ

Puréed spinach gives this lavish soufflé an emerald color through and through. You might serve it with sliced roast turkey and buttery rolls.

- 1 package (10 oz) frozen chopped spinach, thawed and well drained
- ¼ cup whipping cream or half-and-half
- ¼ cup finely chopped shallots or mild onion
- 3 tablespoons butter or margarine
- 2 tablespoons flour
- ½ teaspoon salt
- ⅛ teaspoon each ground nutmeg and dried tarragon
  Pinch cayenne pepper
- ¾ cup milk
- ½ cup each grated Swiss and Cheddar cheese
- 5 eggs, separated

1. Preheat oven to 350° F. Place spinach in blender or food processor with cream. Process until smooth.

2. In a large, heavy saucepan, cook shallots in butter over medium heat, stirring occasionally, until soft but not brown. Stir in flour, salt, nutmeg, tarragon, and cayenne; cook, stirring, until bubbly.

3. Remove from heat and gradually blend in milk, then spinach purée. Return to heat and cook, stirring constantly, until thickened. Mix in cheeses, stirring until they melt. Remove pan from heat and beat in egg yolks, one at a time.

4. Beat egg whites until they form short, distinct peaks. Fold about half the whites thoroughly into the spinach mixture, then gently fold in remaining whites. Pour into a well-buttered 1½-quart soufflé dish. With tip of spatula, draw a circle around circumference of the soufflé about 1 inch in from side of dish.

5. Bake until soufflé is well browned and crust feels firm when tapped lightly (35 to 40 minutes).

Serves 4.

CHEESE-STUFFED BAKED GREEN CHILES

Not as tricky as a soufflé, this *chiles rellenos*-like casserole is delicious for brunch with warm buttered tortillas and grilled sausages.

- 1 can (7 oz) green chiles
- ½ pound Monterey jack or longhorn cheese
- 1 medium onion, finely chopped
- 3 tablespoons flour
- ½ teaspoon baking powder
- ⅛ teaspoon salt
- 3 eggs, separated

1. Preheat oven to 325° F. Slit chiles and carefully remove seeds. Cut cheese into as many strips as there are chiles. Fill chiles with cheese strips and chopped onion; reshape chiles to cover filling. Place them in a single layer in a greased 8-inch square baking pan or shallow 2-quart casserole.

2. Mix flour, baking powder, and salt. Add 1 tablespoon of the egg whites to the egg yolks, then beat egg whites until stiff but not dry. Using the same beater, beat egg yolks until light colored, then beat in flour mixture. Mix in a little of the beaten egg whites to lighten mixture, then fold beaten egg whites into egg yolk mixture. Pour batter over stuffed chiles.

3. Bake until batter is set and top is golden brown (20 to 30 minutes). Serve at once.

Serves 4 to 6.

INDIVIDUAL TOMATO SOUFFLÉS WITH BASIL AND SHRIMP

Here is a very special soufflé for a brunch main dish. Bake it in individual soufflé dishes or in one large one.

- 1 medium onion, finely chopped
- 1½ tablespoons olive oil
- 1 clove garlic, minced or pressed
- 1 large can (28 oz) tomatoes
- 2 tablespoons fresh basil, coarsely chopped, or 1½ teaspoons dried basil
- ½ teaspoon sugar
- 1 teaspoon salt
- ¼ teaspoon pepper
- ¼ pound small peeled, cooked shrimp
- 2 tablespoons each butter and flour
- 1 cup grated Gruyère or Swiss cheese
- 5 eggs, separated

1. Preheat oven to 350° F. In a large saucepan cook onion in olive oil over medium heat until soft but not browned. Mix in garlic, tomatoes (coarsley chopped) and their liquid, basil, sugar, salt, and pepper. Bring to a boil, cover, reduce heat, and simmer for 15 minutes. Uncover and boil gently, stirring occasionally, until tomato mixture is thickened and reduced to about 1¾ cups.

2. Remove ½ cup of the tomato mixture, add shrimp to it, and divide mixture evenly among 4 well-buttered individual 1-cup soufflé dishes (or use a single 1½-quart soufflé dish); set dishes aside.

3. Place remaining tomato mixture in blender or food processor and whirl or process until smooth.

4. Melt butter in a large, heavy saucepan over medium heat. Stir in flour and cook, stirring, until bubbly. Remove from heat and gradually blend in tomato mixture. Return to heat and cook, stirring constantly, until thickened. Add ¾ cup of the cheese and stir until it melts. Remove pan from heat and beat in egg yolks, one at a time.

5. Beat egg whites until they form short, distinct peaks. Fold about half of the whites thoroughly into the tomato mixture, then gently fold in remaining whites. Divide mixture evenly among prepared soufflé dishes. With tip of a spatula, draw a circle around circumference of each soufflé about 1 inch in from side of dish. Sprinkle with remaining ¼ cup cheese.

6. Bake until soufflés are well browned and crust feels firm when tapped lightly (20 to 25 minutes for individual soufflés; 35 to 40 minutes for single soufflé in a 1½-quart dish). Serve at once.

Serves 4.

MUSHROOM SOUFFLÉ WITH TARRAGON

Adding finely chopped mushrooms gives this traditional soufflé yet another new dimension of flavor.

> 6 *tablespoons butter or*
> *margarine*
> 1 *shallot, finely chopped or 2*
> *tablespoons finely chopped*
> *mild onion*
> 6 *ounces mushrooms, finely*
> *chopped*
> 3 *tablespoons flour*
> *Dash cayenne pepper*
> ¼ *teaspoon dry mustard*
> ⅛ *teaspoon ground nutmeg*
> ½ *teaspoon each salt and*
> *dried tarragon*
> 1 *cup milk*
> 1 *cup grated Gruyère or*
> *Swiss cheese*
> ¼ *cup chopped parsley*
> 5 *eggs, separated*

1. Preheat oven to 350° F. In a large, heavy saucepan, melt butter over medium heat. Add shallot and mushrooms and cook, stirring often, until mushrooms brown lightly. Stir in flour, cayenne, dry mustard, nutmeg, salt, and tarragon. Cook, stirring, until bubbly.

2. Remove from heat and gradually blend in milk. Return to heat and cook, stirring constantly, until thickened. Add cheese and parsley and stir until cheese melts. Remove pan from heat and beat in egg yolks, one at a time.

3. Beat egg whites until they form short, distinct peaks. Fold about half of the whites thoroughly into the sauce, then gently fold in remaining whites. Pour into a well-buttered 1½-quart soufflé dish. With the tip of a spatula, draw a circle around circumference of the soufflé about 1 inch in from side of dish.

4. Bake until soufflé is well browned and crust feels firm when tapped lightly (35 to 40 minutes). Serve at once.

Serves 4.

Once you have mastered the technique of soufflé making, all the many types are merely variations on a theme. It is easier than you might think to bake this spectacular Mushroom Soufflé With Tarragon for brunch.

CALVADOS SOUFFLÉ

When you want a really elegant dessert to top off a brunch, consider this tender apple soufflé. It owes much of its flavor to Calvados (pronounce it CAHL-vah-dohs), a brash apple brandy from Normandy. This soufflé, with its custard sauce, tames the fire of the brandy to a sweet, apple-scented warmth.

> *Butter and sugar for soufflé dish*
> ½ *cup sugar*
> ⅓ *cup flour*
> 1⅓ *cups milk*
> 5 *eggs, separated*
> 1 *teaspoon vanilla extract*
> ¼ *cup Calvados (French apple brandy)*
> 2 *teaspoons grated lemon rind*
> 1 *teaspoon grated orange rind*
> 1¼ *cups finely chopped tart green apples (peeled)*
> 2 *tablespoons butter or margarine*
> ⅛ *teaspoon cream of tartar*

Calvados Custard Sauce

> ⅔ *cup milk*
> 2 *egg yolks*
> 3 *tablespoons sugar*
> 1 *teaspoon vanilla extract*
> 2 *tablespoons Calvados*

1. Preheat oven to 400° F. Generously butter a 1½- to 2-quart soufflé dish. Sprinkle with sugar, tipping and shaking to coat evenly. Set aside.

2. Mix the ½ cup sugar and the flour in a large, heavy saucepan. Using a whisk, gradually blend in milk, then egg yolk. Cook, stirring constantly, over medium heat until mixture thickens. Remove from heat and blend in vanilla, 2 tablespoons of the Calvados, and the lemon and orange rinds.

3. In a medium frying pan, cook apples in melted butter with remaining Calvados, stirring over medium heat until tender. Stir apples into egg yolk mixture. (This much can be done several hours ahead; cover lightly and let stand until ready to complete soufflé.)

4. Beat egg whites with cream of tartar until they form short, distinct peaks. Fold about half the whites thoroughly into apple mixture, then gently fold in remaining whites. Pour into prepared soufflé dish.

5. Bake soufflé, placing dish in a large, shallow pan filled to a depth of about 1 inch with hot water, for 25 to 30 minutes, until it is puffy and golden.

6. Serve at once, pouring Calvados Custard Sauce over each portion.

Serves 6.

Calvados Custard Sauce Scald milk in top of double boiler over direct medium heat. Beat egg yolks and sugar in a medium bowl, then gradually beat in scalded milk. Return milk mixture to double boiler over simmering water and cook, stirring constantly, until sauce begins to thicken and coats a metal spoon. Remove from heat and stir in vanilla and Calvados. Serve warm or cooled.

Makes about 1 cup.

ROULADE WITH MUSHROOM FILLING

This *roulade* is a soufflé-like mixture baked in a large, flat pan, then rolled up, jelly-roll fashion, around a filling. Serve these light, moist, mushroom-swirled slices for brunch with a crisp green salad, French bread, and a dry white wine.

> *Butter or margarine for baking pan*
> ¼ *cup butter or margarine*
> ¼ *cup flour*
> *Pinch each ground nutmeg and cayenne pepper*
> ½ *teaspoon salt*
> ¾ *cup milk*
> 6 *eggs, separated*
> ¼ *teaspoon cream of tartar*
> 3 *tablespoons grated Parmesan cheese*
> ½ *cup grated Gruyère or Swiss cheese*

Mushroom Filling

> ¾ *pound mushrooms*
> ¼ *cup butter or margarine*
> ¼ *cup each finely chopped shallots or mild onion and finely chopped ham*
> ¼ *teaspoon each salt and dried tarragon*
> ¼ *cup whipping cream*

1. Preheat oven to 350° F. Butter a 15- by 10-inch shallow baking pan, line bottom with waxed paper, and butter it generously.

2. Melt the ¼ cup butter in a medium saucepan over medium heat. Mix in flour, nutmeg, cayenne, and salt; cook, stirring, until bubbly. Remove from heat and gradually blend in milk. Cook, stirring constantly, until mixture thickens and pulls away from sides of pan.

3. In a large bowl using a wire whisk, beat egg yolks. Gradually blend in thickened sauce. In another large bowl, beat egg whites with cream of tartar until stiff peaks form. Fold egg whites into egg yolk mixture. Spread in prepared pan. Bake until roulade is puffy and surface is firm when pressed lightly (15 to 20 minutes).

4. Invert onto a large sheet of aluminum foil on a baking sheet. Peel off waxed paper. Spread evenly with Mushroom Filling; sprinkle with Parmesan cheese. Starting from a long edge, roll up carefully. Place roll in center of foil. Sprinkle top with Gruyère cheese. Broil, about 4 inches from heat, until cheese is melted and lightly browned (3 to 4 minutes).

Serves 4 to 6.

Mushroom Filling Finely chop mushrooms. In a large frying pan over medium-high heat, melt butter. Add mushrooms, shallots, and ham. Cook, stirring, until liquid is gone and mushrooms brown lightly. Stir in salt, dried tarragon, and cream. Cook, stirring, until most of the liquid is gone.

Makes about 1¾ cups.

This delicate, soufflé-like Roulade With Mushroom Filling is baked first, then filled and rolled. It is finished with a sprinkling of Gruyère cheese.

To make Joe's Special (page 64), add eggs to a savory mixture of well-browned ground beef, onion, mushrooms, and fresh spinach.

Meats, Poultry & Fish

When you think of a hearty breakfast to linger over, it's probably a combination of a savory meat with eggs: crisp strips of bacon with eggs or nuggets of ham in an omelet. These classics have earned a deserved place on anyone's morning menu. But there is no reason to stop there. Enjoy the novelty of fish or shellfish for breakfast, or use leftovers creatively. Potatoes, for many, go with meat whenever possible—even at breakfast. That's why this chapter includes a special feature on the kinds of potatoes one craves in the morning: hashed browns, cottage fries, and crisp skins.

JOE'S SPECIAL

Ground beef for brunch! Why not? Especially when it is browned quickly with onion and mushrooms, then scrambled with spinach and eggs to make a longtime San Francisco favorite—Joe's Special. Serve with a crusty loaf of bread, butter, and a light red wine such as an Italian or California Barbera or Grignolino.

- 1½ tablespoons olive oil
- 1 pound ground beef, crumbled
- 1 large onion, finely chopped
- 1 clove garlic, minced or pressed
- ¼ pound mushrooms, sliced
- 1 teaspoon salt
- ⅛ teaspoon each pepper and dried oregano
  Pinch ground nutmeg
- 2 cups coarsely chopped fresh spinach
- 3 eggs
  Grated Parmesan cheese

1. In a large frying pan over high heat, heat olive oil and brown ground beef well.

2. Add onion, garlic, and mushrooms; reduce heat and continue cooking, stirring occasionally, until onion is soft. Stir in salt, pepper, oregano, nutmeg, and spinach; cook for about 5 minutes longer, stirring several times, until spinach is limp.

3. Reduce heat to low and break eggs over meat mixture; quickly stir just until eggs begin to set. Serve immediately, with cheese to sprinkle over each serving to taste.

Serves 3 to 4.

SWEETBREADS AND MUSHROOMS IN MARSALA CREAM

Spoon these rich creamed sweetbreads over toasted English muffins. Or if you wish to be a bit fancier, bake puff pastry patty shells to hold the sweetbreads. If you like, this can be a buffet dish, served from a chafing dish *bain marie.*

- 1½ pounds sweetbreads
- 1½ teaspoons salt
- 2 tablespoons lemon juice
- ¼ cup butter or margarine
- ½ pound mushrooms, thinly sliced
- 2 tablespoons flour
- ⅛ teaspoon each white pepper and ground nutmeg
- ¾ cup chicken broth, homemade or canned
- 1 cup half-and-half
- 1 egg yolk
- 2 tablespoons dry or sweet Marsala wine
- 6 split English muffins, hot, toasted, and buttered
  Watercress sprigs, for garnish

1. Place sweetbreads in a large, heavy saucepan; sprinkle with 1 teaspoon of the salt. Add water to cover by about 1 inch and 1 tablespoon of the lemon juice. Bring to a boil over medium heat, then reduce heat and simmer, covered, for 15 minutes.

2. Drain sweetbreads, place in a bowl, and cover with cold water. Let stand until cool, changing water several times. Drain and pat dry. Use a small knife to peel membranes and cut out connecting tubes. Separate sweetbreads into bite-sized pieces. (You should have about 3 cups.)

3. In a large frying pan over medium heat, brown sweetbreads lightly in 2 tablespoons of the butter, removing and reserving sweetbreads as they brown. When all are browned, add remaining butter to pan. In it cook mushrooms until lightly

browned. Stir in flour, remaining ½ teaspoon salt, white pepper, and nutmeg and cook until bubbly. Remove from heat and gradually blend in broth and half-and-half.

4. Return to heat and cook, stirring, until thickened and bubbling, then boil gently for 5 minutes. Beat egg yolk in a small bowl; blend in a little of the hot mushroom sauce. Then add egg yolk mixture to remaining mushroom sauce. Cook, stirring, over low heat until thickened and smooth. (Do not boil.)

5. Blend in remaining 1 tablespoon lemon juice and Marsala, then add sweetbreads. Stir gently just until sweetbreads are heated through.

6. Spoon sweetbreads over English muffins. Garnish with watercress.

Serves 6.

GRILLED ITALIAN SAUSAGES WITH PEPPERS

In fair weather or foul, these sausages—grilled outdoors on the barbecue or fried indoors in a frying pan—make a satisfying brunch with Italian or French bread, omelets (page 51) rolled around Fontina or Parmesan cheese, and a sauté of pepper and onions.

- 1½ pounds Italian sausages
- 2 tablespoons each butter or margarine and olive oil
- 1 large onion, thinly slivered
- 1 each sweet red and green bell pepper, seeded and cut in thin strips
- 1 small clove garlic, minced or pressed
- ½ teaspoon each salt and dried oregano
  Freshly ground black pepper
  Lemon wedges and Italian (flat-leaf) parsley, for garnish

1. Pierce each sausage in several places with a fork. Place on grill about 6 inches above a bed of glowing coals. (Or cook on a range-top grill or in a large, heavy frying pan over medium heat.) Cook, turning occasionally, until well browned and cooked in center (20 to 25 minutes). (Juice should run clear when sausage is pierced with a fork.)

2. While sausages are cooking, melt butter with olive oil in a large frying pan over medium heat. Add onion and cook, stirring often, until limp. Mix in peppers, garlic, salt, and oregano. Continue cooking until onions brown lightly and peppers are crisp-tender (about 5 minutes). Grind pepper over mixture to taste.

3. Spoon pepper mixture in center of a warm platter; surround with cooked sausages. Garnish with lemon and parsley.

Serves 4 to 6.

Grilled Italian Sausages With Peppers make a colorful complement for Basic Omelets (recipe on page 51). Tips on how to make the perfect omelet are on page 53.

65

BREAKFAST POTATOES

Go ahead, indulge! Prepare one of these irresistible potato dishes to complement sausages, ham, or bacon with eggs. The Hashed Brown Potatoes are grated, then crisply fried with a touch of onions. Give Cottage Fried Potatoes a down-home appeal by cooking, slicing, and frying them with the skins on. Baked Potato Skins are delicious as is, or as containers for scrambled or poached eggs.

HASHED BROWN POTATOES

> 5   *medium potatoes*
>   *(about 2 lbs)*
> ¼   *cup finely chopped onion*
> ½   *teaspoon salt*
>   *Pinch white pepper*
> 2   *tablespoons* each *butter or*
>   *margarine and salad oil*

1. Cook potatoes, in their jackets, in boiling salted water until about half cooked (15 to 20 minutes). When cool enough to handle, slip off skins. Shred potatoes coarsely into a bowl. Mix lightly with onion, salt, and white pepper.

2. In a heavy, well-seasoned or nonstick 9- to 10-inch frying pan over medium heat, melt butter with 1 tablespoon of the oil. Add potatoes, pressing down with a spatula. Cook over low heat (without stirring) until potatoes are brown and crusty on bottom (12 to 15 minutes).

3. Loosen edges with a spatula. Cover pan with a plate, invert potatoes onto it, and add remaining tablespoon oil to pan. Swirl to coat pan well. Slide potatoes back into pan and cook until bottom is well browned and crusty (12 to 15 minutes).

4. Serve from pan or invert onto a warm serving plate.

Serves 6.

COTTAGE FRIED POTATOES

> 5   *medium potatoes*
>   *(about 2 lbs)*
> 2   *tablespoons* each *butter or*
>   *margarine and salad oil*
> ⅛   *teaspoon paprika*
>   *Salt and coarsely ground*
>   *pepper*

1. Scrub potatoes well. Cook, in their jackets, in boiling salted water until about half cooked (15 to 20 minutes). Without peeling, slice potatoes about ⅛ inch thick.

2. In a large, heavy frying pan over medium-low heat, melt butter with oil and paprika. Add potatoes. Sprinkle lightly with salt and pepper.

3. Cook, using a wide spatula to lift and turn potatoes occasionally, until they are brown and crusty on all sides (20 to 25 minutes). Turn carefully to keep slices from breaking.

Serves 4 to 6.

BAKED POTATO SKINS

> 6   *small baking potatoes*
>   *(4 to 5 in. long)*
> ¼   *cup butter or margarine*
> ¼   *teaspoon paprika*
>   *Pinch white pepper*

1. Preheat oven to 400° F. Scrub potatoes, pat dry, and rub skins lightly with a little of the butter. Pierce potatoes in several places with a fork.

2. Bake potatoes until tender when pierced (45 minutes to 1 hour). When cool enough to handle, cut in halves and scoop out potato, leaving a thin shell about ⅛ inch thick. Reserve potato for other dishes (see Fisherman's Pie, page 78).

3. Place skins on a baking sheet. Melt butter in a small pan with paprika and white pepper. Stir. Brush insides of potato skins with butter mixture.

4. Bake potato skins until crisp and golden (18 to 20 minutes). (Try adding grated Cheddar cheese, crumbled bacon, green onion, or chives.)

Serves 6.

KAREN'S HAM AND SPINACH ROLLS

Here is an easy and very elegant brunch dish that will serve 8 to 10. Thinly sliced ham is rolled around a filling that combines spinach, sour cream, and cornbread stuffing mix. Topped with a robust cheese sauce, it can be made ahead, refrigerated, then baked later. As accompaniments, serve a molded carrot and pineapple salad, sesame seed rolls, and if wine is in order, a crisp, dry rosé.

> 2 packages (10 oz each) frozen chopped spinach, thawed
> 2 cups sour cream
> ¼ teaspoon ground nutmeg
> 2 cups packaged cornbread stuffing mix
> 20 thin slices (about 1¼ lbs) baked or boiled ham
> ½ cup grated Parmesan cheese

Nippy Cheese Sauce

> 2 tablespoons butter or margarine
> 2 tablespoons flour
> ⅛ teaspoon cayenne pepper
> 1½ cups milk
> 1 cup grated sharp Cheddar cheese
> 1 tablespoon dry sherry

1. Drain spinach in a colander, pressing out moisture. In a large bowl stir together spinach, sour cream, and nutmeg. Blend in stuffing mix.

2. Place about ¼ cup of the spinach mixture on each ham slice, rolling them up and placing side by side in a buttered shallow 3-quart baking dish (about 9 by 13 inches).

3. Pour Nippy Cheese Sauce evenly over ham rolls. Sprinkle with Parmesan cheese. If made ahead, cover and refrigerate.

4. Preheat oven to 350° F. Bake, covered, for 15 minutes. Uncover and bake until sauce is bubbly and lightly browned (15 to 20 minutes; add 5 to 10 minutes to baking time if made ahead).

Serves 8 to 10.

Nippy Cheese Sauce In a medium saucepan over moderate heat, melt butter. Stir in flour and cayenne; cook until bubbly. Remove from heat and gradually blend in milk. Return to heat and cook, stirring, until thickened and bubbly. Stir in cheese until melted, then mix in sherry.

Makes about 2 cups.

DILLED CORNED BEEF HASH

Try this irresistible dish with rye toast and mugs of strong, steaming coffee.

> ½ cup butter or margarine
> 2 large onions, finely chopped
> ½ teaspoon sugar
> 2 medium potatoes, cooked, peeled, and diced
> 3 to 4 cups cooked corned beef brisket, cut in ½-inch cubes
> ½ teaspoon dried dillweed
> ⅛ teaspoon pepper
> 4 to 6 warm poached eggs (optional; see page 44)
>   Dill sprigs or chopped parsley, for garnish

1. In a large, heavy frying pan over medium heat, melt ¼ cup of the butter until foamy. Add onions and sugar; cook slowly, stirring occasionally, until onions are soft and golden (about 20 minutes).

2. Swirl in 2 tablespoons more of the butter, then lightly mix in potatoes, corned beef, dillweed, and pepper. Press mixture down lightly with a spatula. Cook over medium heat until bottom of hash is golden brown (about 10 minutes).

3. Loosen hash with spatula. Cover pan with a large plate and invert hash onto plate. Add remaining 2 tablespoons butter to pan and swirl until melted. Slide hash back into pan, browned side up. Continue cooking slowly until bottom is golden brown (10 to 15 minutes).

4. Again invert hash onto plate. Use a spoon to make 4 to 6 hollows in hash and slip a poached egg into each (if used). Garnish with dill sprigs.

Serves 4 to 6.

MAKE YOUR OWN PORK SAUSAGE

Pork butt often contains a generous proportion of fat. Trim off some of it if you prefer a leaner sausage—but *not* all of it. Fat makes the sausage juicy and carries the flavors of the seasonings. Grind the meat, using a food chopper or food processor, then mix in savory seasonings.

PORK SAUSAGE

> 2 pounds boneless pork butt, cut in 1-inch cubes
> 1 clove garlic, minced or pressed
> 1½ teaspoons dried sage
> 1 teaspoon salt
> ½ teaspoon each *dried summer savory or marjoram and coarsely ground black pepper*
> ¼ teaspoon each *ground allspice and dried thyme*
> ⅛ teaspoon cayenne pepper

1. Using coarse blade of food chopper, grind pork cubes twice. Or, to use food processor for grinding meat, first spread pork cubes in a single layer on a baking sheet and place in freezer until meat is firm but not frozen (about 20 minutes). Then process, using short on-off bursts, until meat is coarsely ground.

2. Using mortar and pestle or blender, combine garlic, sage, salt, summer savory, black pepper, allspice, thyme, and cayenne pepper thoroughly. Add to ground meat and mix well until seasonings are evenly distributed. (Use your hands if you wish.)

3. Wrap well and refrigerate for 8 hours or overnight to blend flavors.

4. Form into patties and cook in a frying pan over medium-low heat until well browned and crusty, or use in recipes as directed.

Makes 2 pounds.

Combine Custardy Baked Sausage Sandwiches with fresh fruits and vegetables to make a winning Sunday family brunch. For an extra treat, add one of the special beverage recipes beginning on page 12.

CUSTARDY BAKED SAUSAGE SANDWICHES

This fine brunch dish must be assembled ahead and refrigerated in order to become puffy and crisp when it is baked. Try it with crisp raw vegetables and a tart fruit sherbet.

    8 slices cracked wheat bread
       Coarse-grained Dijon mustard
    1 pound bulk pork sausage,
       crumbled
    1 small onion, finely chopped
    1 cup grated Swiss cheese
    4 eggs
    ½ cup sour cream
    ¾ teaspoon salt
       Pinch each *white pepper and
       ground nutmeg*
    2 cups milk
       Paprika

1. Trim crusts from bread if you wish. Spread half of the slices lightly with mustard. Place, mustard side up, in a well-buttered 8- or 9-inch square baking dish.

2. In a medium frying pan over medium heat, cook sausage and onion in sausage drippings, stirring occasionally, until sausage is lightly browned. Using a slotted spoon, spoon sausage mixture evenly over bread slices in baking dish. Sprinkle evenly with cheese. Cover with remaining bread slices.

3. In a medium bowl beat eggs with sour cream, salt, white pepper, and nutmeg. Gradually beat in milk until well blended. Pour egg mixture slowly and evenly over top of bread slices. Sprinkle lightly with paprika. Cover and refrigerate for at least 1 hour (or as long as overnight).

4. Preheat oven to 325° F. Bake, uncovered, until sandwiches are puffed and custard is set in center (45 minutes to 1 hour).

Serves 4.

LAMB CAKES

If, for brunch, you would like to accompany a vegetable omelet, quiche, or crêpes with an interesting meat, try these ground lamb patties. They are served with a colorful hot garnish of pimientos and parsley.

    1 egg
    ¼ cup soft bread crumbs
    ½ teaspoon garlic salt
    ⅛ teaspoon ground cinnamon
    1 jar (4 oz) pimientos, drained
       and finely chopped
    1 pound ground lean lamb
    1 tablespoon each *butter or
       margarine and olive oil*
    1 teaspoon lemon juice
    1 tablespoon water
    ¼ cup chopped parsley

1. In a medium bowl beat egg slightly, then mix in crumbs, garlic salt, cinnamon, and ¼ cup of the chopped pimientos. Lightly mix in lamb; shape mixture into 8 flat patties.

2. In a large frying pan over medium heat, melt butter with oil; brown lamb patties slowly, turning once and cooking about 6 minutes on each side. Remove patties to a warm serving dish and keep them warm.

3. Pour off and discard all but about 1 tablespoon of the pan drippings. Add remaining pimientos, lemon juice, water, and parsley. Cook, stirring to incorporate brown bits from pan, just until mixture is heated through. Spoon over lamb patties.

Serves 4.

YANKEE CLIPPER CHICKEN

Accompany this hearty New England brunch dish with fluffy homemade biscuits and honey.

> 1 *frying chicken (3 to 3½ lbs),*
>   *cut in quarters*
>   *Salt, white pepper, ground*
>   *nutmeg, and flour*
> 1 *tablespoon each butter or*
>   *margarine and salad oil*
> 4 *carrots, sliced ¼ inch thick*
> 1 *onion, thinly sliced*
> ½ *cup chopped celery*
> ¼ *cup each chicken broth and*
>   *dry vermouth or dry sherry*

1. Preheat oven to 325° F. Sprinkle chicken lightly on all sides with salt, white pepper, and nutmeg; then coat lightly with flour, shaking off excess. In a large, heavy frying pan over medium heat, melt butter with oil; in it brown chicken well on all sides. As chicken browns, remove quarters and place in a single layer, skin side up, in a 10-inch square casserole.

2. Pour off and discard all but about 1 tablespoon of the drippings. Add carrots, onion, and celery; cook, stirring, until onion is tender and lightly browned. Add chicken broth and vermouth; stir to incorporate pan drippings. Pour vegetable mixture over chicken.

3. Cover and bake until chicken and vegetables are tender (about 1 hour). Uncover and bake for 10 to 15 minutes longer, until chicken is brown and crisp.

4. Spoon vegetables and sauce over chicken before serving.

Serves 4.

Lamb Cakes, topped with colorful pimientos and parsley, make a good brunch accompaniment to meatless quiches, crêpes, or omelets.

Split homemade brioches and fill them with creamy chicken seasoned with tarragon. Instructions for making brioches are given on page 108.

CHICKEN TARRAGON–FILLED BRIOCHES

For those who enjoy baking, buttery brioches make a fine medium for this creamy chicken, but it can also be served over fluffy rice. If you make the chicken sauce in advance, cover and refrigerate it; then reheat, stirring gently, in a double boiler over simmering water.

> 1 frying chicken (3½ to 4 lbs), cut up
> Salt, ground white pepper, and nutmeg
> 3 tablespoons butter
> ¼ cup finely chopped shallots or mild onion
> 1½ teaspoons dried tarragon
> ⅓ cup chopped parsley
> 1½ cups dry white wine
> ¾ cup whipping cream
> 1 egg yolk
> 6 warm brioches (see page 108)
> 1 avocado, peeled and cut in wedges, for garnish
> Cherry tomatoes, for garnish

1. Sprinkle chicken pieces lightly with salt, white pepper, and nutmeg. In a large, heavy frying pan, heat butter and brown chicken lightly on all sides.

2. Add shallots, tarragon, parsley, and wine. Bring to a boil, cover, reduce heat, and simmer until chicken is very tender (1 hour). Remove chicken and reserve cooking liquid remaining in pan.

3. Remove chicken from bones, discarding skin and bones; cut into bite-sized pieces.

4. Add cream to cooking liquid and bring to a boil. Boil, stirring occasionally, until reduced by about a fourth. Remove from heat. Beat egg yolk in a small bowl; blend a little of the hot liquid with yolk, then return all to pan and stir. Mix in chicken. Cook, stirring lightly, over low heat until sauce thickens slightly. (Do not boil after adding egg yolk.) Taste, and add salt if needed.

5. Cut brioches to—but not through—bottom crusts into quarters; spread open carefully on individual plates. Spoon hot chicken mixture into brioches. Garnish with avocado wedges and cherry tomatoes.

Serves 6.

LEMONY CREAMED TURKEY IN FRENCH ROLLS

Hollow out and toast rectangular or round French rolls to make containers for this delicious turkey, caper, and ripe olive filling. Add cranberry-orange relish for a sweet-sour flavor contrast.

- 4 sourdough French rolls, about 5½ by 3½ inches, or 4 inches in diameter
- ½ cup butter or margarine
- 1 teaspoon lemon juice
- ⅛ teaspoon paprika
- 1 small clove garlic, minced or pressed (optional)
- 3 green onions, thinly sliced (use part of tops)
- 3 tablespoons flour
- ½ teaspoon salt
  Pinch white pepper
- 1½ cups half-and-half
- 1 teaspoon Dijon mustard
- ⅔ cup dry white wine
- 2 cups diced cooked turkey
- ⅓ cup sliced ripe olives
- 1 tablespoon drained capers
- 1 teaspoon grated lemon rind
  Thinly sliced green onions, for garnish

1. Preheat oven to 325° F. Cut off tops of French rolls, then scoop out each bottom to make a ½-inch-thick case. (Save tops and insides to make bread crumbs for use in other recipes.) Melt ¼ cup of the butter in a small pan with lemon juice, paprika, and garlic (if used). Brush insides of rolls with butter mixture, and place on a baking sheet.

2. Bake, uncovered, until rolls are crisp and insides are golden brown (20 to 25 minutes). Keep warm.

3. In a large, heavy saucepan, melt remaining ¼ cup butter over medium heat. Add the 3 sliced green onions and cook just until limp. Stir in flour, salt, and white pepper; cook, stirring until thickened.

4. Remove flour mixture from heat and gradually blend in half-and-half and mustard. Cook, stirring until thickened.

5. Blend in wine, then mix in turkey, olives, capers, and lemon rind. Cook, stirring occasionally, a few minutes longer until heated through.

6. To serve, spoon creamed turkey evenly into and over warm, toasted French rolls. Sprinkle with sliced green onions.

Serves 4.

MAPLE BAKED CHICKEN

The slightly sweet flavor of this baked chicken topped with crisp almonds makes it a good choice for brunch with rice and fresh peas.

- ¼ cup butter or margarine
- 1 frying chicken (3 lbs), cut up
- ¼ cup slivered blanched almonds
- ¼ cup maple syrup
- 1 teaspoon salt
  Dash each ground nutmeg and white pepper
- ½ teaspoon grated lemon rind
- 2 teaspoons lemon juice

1. While heating oven to 350° F, place butter in a shallow baking dish and heat in oven until butter is melted and bubbling.

2. Place chicken pieces, skin side down, in melted butter; then turn skin side up. Sprinkle chicken with almonds. Combine maple syrup with remaining ingredients; pour evenly over chicken.

3. Bake, uncovered, drizzling occasionally with cooking liquid, until chicken is well browned and tests done at thickest parts (about 1 hour).

Serves 4 to 5.

TURKEY HASH WITH CURRY SAUCE

A good post-holiday brunch dish, this hash goes well with a molded cranberry salad and rolls.

- ¼ cup butter or margarine
- 1 medium onion, thinly slivered
- 1 small sweet red or green bell pepper, seeded and finely chopped
- ¼ teaspoon paprika
- 4 cups diced cooked turkey
- 1 medium potato, cooked, peeled, and diced
- ¼ cup golden raisins
- ½ teaspoon salt
  Pinch white pepper

Curry Sauce

- 2 tablespoons butter
- 1 teaspoon Indian curry powder
- 2 tablespoons flour
- ¼ teaspoon each salt and dry mustard
- 1 cup chicken broth
- ¾ cup milk
- ½ teaspoon grated lemon rind

1. In a 10-inch frying pan over medium heat, melt butter and cook onion and bell pepper, stirring until soft but not brown. Mix in paprika.

2. Lightly mix in turkey, potato, raisins, salt, and white pepper. Press down lightly with a spatula. Continue cooking over medium heat until hash is heated through and a golden brown crust forms on bottom (10 to 12 minutes).

3. Loosen hash with a spatula. Invert onto warm serving plate. Serve with Curry Sauce.

Serves 4 to 6.

Curry Sauce In a medium saucepan over moderate heat, melt butter. Stir in curry powder, then flour, salt, and mustard. Cook and stir until bubbly. Remove from heat and gradually blend in chicken broth and milk. Add lemon rind. Cook, stirring constantly, until thickened; then cook, stirring occasionally, for 2 minutes.

Makes about 2 cups.

TAILGATE BRUNCH

*Bloody Marys
(see page 25)*

*Ham in Rye Buns With
Mustard Sauce*

Crisp Raw Vegetables

Mixed Pickles

Shredded-Apple Cake

Pears

Coffee

Arrive at the stadium early enough to avoid parking hassles, and you will have plenty of time before an afternoon game for a late-morning brunch. Yeasty homemade rye rolls filled with ground ham make an unusual hot sandwich.

To serve them hot on game day, bake the rolls a day or more ahead and refrigerate or freeze them; reheat, lightly covered, in a 325° F oven, then wrap well.

HAM IN RYE BUNS WITH MUSTARD SAUCE

- 1 package active dry yeast
- 1 cup warm (110° to 115° F) water
- ¼ cup sugar
- ½ teaspoon salt
- ½ cup butter or margarine, softened
- 3 cups all-purpose flour
- 1 egg
- ½ cup rye flour
- ¼ cup salad oil

Ground Ham Filling

- 2 tablespoons butter or margarine
- 1 small onion, finely chopped
- 1 clove garlic, minced or pressed
- 3 cups ground cooked smoked ham
- ½ cup sour cream
- ¼ teaspoon ground cloves

Dilled Mustard Sauce

- ¼ cup butter or margarine
- 3 tablespoons flour
- ½ teaspoon each salt and dried dillweed
- ⅛ teaspoon white pepper
- 1 tablespoon Dijon mustard
- 2 cups milk
- 1 egg yolk
- 2 tablespoons lemon juice

1. Sprinkle yeast over water in large bowl of an electric mixer; let stand about 5 minutes to soften. Stir in sugar, salt, and butter, mixing until butter melts. Add 2½ cups of the all-purpose flour. Mix to blend, then beat 5 minutes at medium speed. Beat in egg, then vigorously mix in remaining ½ cup all-purpose flour and rye flour until well combined.

2. Place batter in a greased bowl, cover, and let rise in a warm place until doubled in bulk (about 1 hour). Punch down, turn dough out on a generously floured board or pastry cloth, and roll to a 16- by 12-inch rectangle. Cut dough into twelve 4-inch squares. Place about ¼ cup filling in center of each square. Bring opposite corners together and pinch to seal.

3. Measure 1 teaspoon oil into each of twelve 2½-inch muffin cups. Place each square of filled dough in a muffin cup and turn to coat with oil, ending with pinched side down.

4. Let rise until buns are puffy (45 minutes to 1 hour). Preheat oven to 400° F. Bake until well browned (20 to 25 minutes). Serve hot with Dilled Mustard Sauce.

Serves 12.

Ground Ham Filling In a medium frying pan melt butter and cook onion until soft but not brown. Mix in garlic, and cook for 1 minute longer. Remove from heat and mix in ham, sour cream, and ground cloves.

Dilled Mustard Sauce In a heavy, medium-sized saucepan over medium heat, melt butter. Mix in flour, salt, dillweed, and white pepper. Cook, stirring, until bubbly. Remove from heat and blend in mustard, then gradually stir in milk. Cook, stirring constantly, until thickened and bubbling. Beat egg yolk in a small bowl; gradually blend in a little of the sauce. Add lemon juice and return to mixture in pan. Cook over low heat, stirring, just until thickened and smooth. (Do not boil.)

Makes about 2⅓ cups.

SHREDDED-APPLE CAKE

- ½ cup butter or margarine, softened
- 2 cups sugar
- 1 teaspoon vanilla extract
- 2 eggs (at room temperature)
- 2 cups flour
- 1½ teaspoons baking soda
- ½ teaspoon ground nutmeg
- 1 cup finely chopped walnuts
- 2 tart apples, peeled, cored, and shredded
  Confectioners' sugar
  Whipped cream (optional)

1. Preheat oven to 325° F. In large bowl of electric mixer, cream butter, sugar, and vanilla until fluffy. Add eggs, one at a time, beating well after each addition.

2. Mix flour, soda, and nutmeg. Add half the flour mixture to butter mixture and beat well. Gradually mix in remaining flour, beating well after the last addition. Fold in nuts and apples.

3. Spread batter in a well-greased, lightly floured 8½- to 9-inch bundt pan or other 9-cup tube pan.

4. Bake until cake tests done when a long skewer is inserted in thickest part (1 hour and 10 to 15 minutes). Let cool in pan for 10 minutes, then invert cake onto a wire rack.

5. Sift confectioners' sugar over top. Serve warm or cool, with whipped cream, if desired.

Serves 8 to 10.

Spread out on the tailgate for a late-morning brunch is Ham in Rye Buns With Mustard Sauce, served warm with crisp raw vegetables, followed by Shredded-Apple Cake.

*To make the most of kip-
pered salmon, combine it
with curried rice in Ked-
geree. Serve for brunch
with toast and tea.*

KEDGEREE

This curiously named Anglo-Indian
creation combines curry-seasoned
rice, smoked salmon or haddock
(finnan haddie), and hard-cooked
eggs to make an irresistible brunch
dish. Indigenous flavors that seem to
team naturally with Kedgeree are
those of breakfast tea and toast with
tomato preserves or marmalade.

> ¼ *cup butter*
> 1 *small onion, finely chopped*
> ¾ *teaspoon Indian curry powder*
> 1 *cup long-grain or California
>   pearl rice*
> ½ *teaspoon salt*
> 2 *cups water*

> ¾ *pound kippered (smoked)
>   salmon or haddock*
> 2 *tablespoons flour
>   Pinch white pepper*
> 1½ *cups chicken broth, canned
>   or homemade*
> 3 *hard-cooked eggs
>   (see page 41)
>   Finely chopped parsley,
>   for garnish*

1. In a large, heavy frying pan over
medium heat, melt 2 tablespoons of
the butter and cook onion until soft
but not brown. Stir in curry powder
and rice until well combined. Sprinkle with salt. Add water, cover, reduce
heat, and simmer until rice is tender
and liquid is absorbed (20 to 25
minutes).

2. Steam fish on a rack over gently
boiling water until it separates easily
into flakes (10 to 15 minutes). Flake
fish, reserving a few large pieces for
garnish; keep warm.

3. In a medium saucepan melt remaining 2 tablespoons butter over
moderate heat. Add flour and white
pepper, stirring until bubbly. Remove
from heat and gradually blend in
chicken broth. Cook, stirring, until
thickened and bubbling. Then boil
gently, stirring occasionally, until
reduced to about 1 cup.

4. Cut eggs in halves. Shred yolks
and whites separately.

5. Into the cooked rice, mix flaked
fish and sauce. Spoon into a warm
serving dish. Top with reserved pieces
of fish and shredded eggs. Sprinkle
with parsley.

Serves 4 to 6.

BROILED KIPPERS WITH SWEET-SOUR ONIONS

Sturdy British breakfasts often include these smoked, salted fish, dotted with butter and broiled in a jiffy. Suitable accompaniments are broiled tomato halves (along with kippers) with herb butter, toast, and a breakfast tea.

> 2 kippered herring (each about 6 oz), butterflied
> 3 tablespoons butter or margarine
> 1 large onion, thinly sliced and separated into rings
> ½ teaspoon mustard seed, coarsely crushed
> 1 teaspoon sugar
> 1 tablespoon raspberry or red wine vinegar
> Freshly ground pepper

1. To remove some of the salt, place herring in a baking dish, pour on boiling water to cover, and let stand for 10 to 15 minutes. Drain herring and pat dry.

2. Preheat broiler. In a large frying pan over medium-low heat, melt 2 tablespoons of the butter and cook onion until limp. Stir in mustard seed and sugar and continue cooking, stirring occasionally, until onions are golden (about 10 minutes).

3. Place herring, opened out, with skin side down, on rack of broiler pan, and dot with remaining 1 tablespoon butter. Broil, about 4 inches from heat, until fish are hot and bubbling (6 to 8 minutes). (You don't need to turn fish.)

4. Just before serving, add vinegar to onions, stirring to deglaze the pan and reduce most of the liquid. Divide onions between each of 2 warm plates. Place a broiled herring beside onions on each plate. Sprinkle pepper over all.

Serves 2.

SCALLOPS IN TOMATO CREAM

Baked in scallop shells or ramekins, scallops with the Provençal touch of a creamy fresh tomato sauce make an unexpected brunch entrée. Serve with rice or a loaf of good bread and a delicate green salad.

> ¼ cup butter or margarine
> 1 pound scallops, thawed if frozen
> ¼ cup finely chopped shallots or mild onion
> ½ pound mushrooms, thinly sliced
> 1 large tomato, peeled and chopped
> 1 teaspoon tomato paste
> ⅓ cup dry white wine
> ½ teaspoon each salt and dried tarragon
> ⅛ teaspoon white pepper
> ½ cup whipping cream
> 2 tablespoons chopped parsley
> ½ cup grated Gruyère cheese

1. Preheat oven to 400° F. In a large frying pan over medium-high heat, melt butter and brown scallops lightly, removing them as they brown and dividing them evenly into 4 buttered baking shells or shallow individual casseroles.

2. In the same pan cook shallots and mushrooms, stirring frequently, until shallots are tender and mushrooms are lightly browned. Mix in tomato, tomato paste, wine, salt, tarragon, and white pepper. Bring to a boil, cover, reduce heat, and simmer 10 minutes.

3. Uncover, stir in cream, and bring to a boil over high heat. Cook, stirring, until sauce is reduced and slightly thickened. Remove from heat and mix in parsley. Spoon sauce over scallops. Sprinkle evenly with cheese.

4. Bake until sauce bubbles and begins to brown at edges (about 10 minutes).

Serves 4.

CRUSTY OYSTER GRATIN

To warm those wintry "R" months, serve these butter-crusted baked oysters for brunch with a marinated broccoli salad, hard rolls, a dry white wine such as Muscadet, and a hot apple or pear dessert.

> ½ cup butter
> Pinch each dried thyme and cayenne pepper
> 2 jars (10 oz each) small oysters
> 1 cup finely crushed soda cracker crumbs
> 2 tablespoons finely chopped parsley

1. Preheat oven to 400° F. Melt butter with thyme and cayenne in a small frying pan.

2. Drain oysters and pat dry. Sprinkle a well-buttered, shallow, 1½- to 2-quart baking dish evenly with half of the cracker crumbs. Dip oysters into melted butter mixture to coat. Arrange oysters in a single layer over crumbs in baking dish. Sprinkle with parsley, then cover with remaining cracker crumbs. Drizzle with butter remaining in frying pan.

3. Bake, uncovered, until crumbs are crisp and brown (15 to 18 minutes).

Serves 4.

If you like fish in the morning, you can't beat Baked Stuffed Trout and warm corn sticks. Conclude with summer-fresh berries and cream.

BAKED STUFFED TROUT

This is a delicious fisherman's breakfast, starring freshly caught brook trout. But even if you do not catch your own and must rely on a fish market for the trout, it still makes a delicious morning meal.

- ¼ cup butter or margarine
- 1 medium onion, finely chopped
- 1 stalk celery, finely chopped
- 1 clove garlic, minced or pressed
- ½ teaspoon salt
- ¼ teaspoon dried tarragon
- ⅛ teaspoon lemon pepper
- ¼ cup finely chopped parsley
- 3 cups cubed firm bread
- 1 egg
- 1 tablespoon dry white wine
- 4 whole trout (about 8 oz each), cleaned
  Salt
- 1 tablespoon each lemon juice and soy sauce
  Flour
- 2 slices bacon, cut in halves crosswise

1. Preheat oven to 350° F. In a large frying pan over medium heat, melt butter and cook onion and celery until soft and lightly browned. Remove from heat and mix in garlic, the ½ teaspoon salt, tarragon, lemon pepper, parsley, and bread. Beat egg with wine; mix lightly with bread mixture. Spread evenly in a shallow, buttered baking dish just large enough to hold trout.

2. Wipe trout, inside and out, with a damp paper towel. Sprinkle with salt. Mix lemon juice and soy sauce; brush cavities of trout with mixture. Coat trout lightly with flour; arrange over stuffing. Drizzle with any remaining soy-lemon mixture. Cover each fish with a half-slice of bacon.

3. Cover and bake until fish are firm (about 45 minutes). Uncover and continue baking until bacon is crisp and brown (10 to 15 minutes).

Serves 4.

SHAD ROE WITH CAPER BUTTER

Shad roe, the pouch-shaped eggs of a saltwater fish that spawns in coastal rivers, is a spring treat for those who appreciate its delicate flavor and unique texture. It makes an elegant breakfast for two, served on toast triangles in a simple lemon, caper, and butter sauce with a fine dry white wine. You might go all out and make the wine Champagne. Curls of crisply fried bacon or frizzled ham also taste good with the fish.

- 1 set (about ¾ lb) shad roe
  Salt, white pepper, and flour
- ¼ cup butter or margarine
- 1 tablespoon each lemon juice and drained capers
  Buttered toast triangles
  Lemon wedges and parsley sprigs, for garnish

1. Rinse shad roe (without separating the 2 halves if possible) and pat dry. Sprinkle with salt and pepper, then coat lightly with flour.

2. In a medium frying pan over moderate heat, melt 2 tablespoons of the butter. Add shad roe and cook, turning once, until roe are nicely browned on both sides and look opaque. (Test center of each half with a small knife.) Remove from pan, separate into halves, and keep warm.

3. To pan add remaining 2 tablespoons butter and lemon juice, swirling and stirring in pan drippings until mixture bubbles. Mix in capers.

4. Place roe on buttered toast triangles on warm plates, pour caper butter over, and garnish with lemon wedges and parsley.

Serves 2.

LOBSTER PIE

This "pie" is really a sherried lobster casserole baked with a topping of crisp crumbs. Use crab in place of lobster if you wish. For brunch, add buttered whole green beans and whole wheat or bran muffins.

- 3 tablespoons butter or margarine
- ¼ cup finely chopped onion
- 3 tablespoons flour
- ¼ teaspoon each salt and paprika
  Pinch white pepper
- 2 cups half-and-half
- 2 tablespoons dry sherry
- 1 teaspoon Worcestershire sauce
- 1 tablespoon lemon juice
- 2 tablespoons chopped parsley
- 1 pound (about 3 cups) cooked lobster or crabmeat

Bread Crumb Topping

- 2 tablespoons butter or margarine
- ⅛ teaspoon paprika
- 1½ cups soft bread crumbs

1. Preheat oven to 400° F. Melt butter in a heavy 2- to 3-quart saucepan over medium heat. Stir in onion and cook until soft but not browned. Stir in flour, salt, paprika, and white pepper; cook until bubbling. Remove from heat and gradually blend in half-and-half, then sherry. Return to medium-low heat and cook, stirring constantly, until thickened and bubbly.

2. Fold in Worcestershire sauce, lemon juice, parsley, and lobster. Spread in a buttered, shallow, 5- to 6-cup casserole. Sprinkle evenly with Bread Crumb Topping.

3. Bake, uncovered, until bread crumbs are brown and crisp (15 to 20 minutes).

Serves 4.

Bread Crumb Topping In a small frying pan melt butter with paprika. Stir in bread crumbs.

HANGTOWN FRY

Dating back to California Gold Rush days, this classic Western oyster, bacon, and egg dish is a sort of frittata.

> 6 slices bacon, cut in halves
> ¼ cup butter or margarine
> 1 jar (10 oz) small oysters
> 6 eggs
>   Flour
> ⅓ cup fine dry bread crumbs
> 1 tablespoon water
> ½ teaspoon salt
>   Pinch white pepper
> 1 tablespoon finely chopped parsley

1. In a 10-inch nonstick frying pan, cook bacon until crisp and brown; remove bacon, drain, and keep warm. Discard bacon drippings. To pan add 3 tablespoons of the butter, swirling until melted.

2. While bacon cooks, drain oysters and pat dry. Beat 1 of the eggs in a medium bowl. Coat oysters first with flour, then with egg, and finally with bread crumbs. Add oysters to melted butter in pan and cook over medium-low heat until brown on first side. Turn to brown second side.

3. As oysters brown, add to the egg in which oysters were dipped the remaining 5 eggs, water, salt, and white pepper. Beat until frothy and well combined (about 30 seconds). After turning oysters, sprinkle with parsley, and then pour beaten eggs into frying pan.

4. Cook as for a frittata (see page 54), lifting and tipping pan as eggs begin to set. When eggs are nearly set, cover pan with a large plate, invert eggs and oysters onto it, and add remaining 1 tablespoon butter to pan. Swirl until melted. Slide eggs back into pan and cook until bottom is lightly browned.

5. Cut in wedges and serve from pan, or invert onto a warm serving plate and cut in wedges. Accompany with bacon.

Serves 4.

FISHERMAN'S PIE

Mounds of cheese-crusted mashed potatoes give this creamy seafood combination—salmon and tiny shrimp—the air of a seafaring shepherd's pie. If fresh salmon fillet is not available, canned salmon (drained and flaked) will serve.

> 4 medium potatoes (about 1½ lbs)
> 1 pound salmon fillets
> ¼ pound mushrooms, thinly sliced
> ¼ cup butter or margarine
> ½ cup thawed frozen peas
> ¼ cup chopped parsley
> ¼ pound tiny peeled, cooked shrimp
> ¼ teaspoon salt
>   Pinch each white pepper and ground nutmeg
> 2 to 3 tablespoons milk or cream
> 1 cup grated Cheddar cheese

Creamy Sauce

> 3 tablespoons butter or margarine
> 3 tablespoons flour
> ¼ teaspoon salt
>   Pinch each white pepper and ground nutmeg
> 2 cups half-and-half
> ⅔ cup grated Swiss cheese

1. Preheat oven to 400° F. Peel potatoes and cut lengthwise into quarters. Cook in boiling salted water until tender (about 20 minutes).

2. Place salmon on a rack above about ½ inch of water in a medium frying pan. Bring water to a boil, cover, reduce heat, and steam until salmon flakes when tested with a fork (6 to 8 minutes). Separate salmon into bite-sized chunks, removing and discarding any bones or skin.

3. In a medium frying pan, cook mushrooms in 2 tablespoons of the butter until lightly browned.

4. Into Creamy Sauce fold salmon, mushrooms, peas, parsley, and shrimp. Spread in a buttered, shallow, 2- to 2½-quart baking dish.

5. Drain cooked potatoes well. Add remaining 2 tablespoons butter, salt, white pepper, and nutmeg. Beat, adding milk gradually, until potatoes are fluffy. Spread potatoes lightly around edges of fish mixture in casserole, *or* drop potatoes by small spoonfuls, *or* pipe through a pastry bag, using a large star tip. Sprinkle cheese evenly over all. (If made ahead, cover and refrigerate.)

6. Bake, uncovered, until potatoes brown lightly and sauce is bubbling (20 to 30 minutes).

Serves 6.

Creamy Sauce In a large, heavy saucepan over medium heat, melt butter. Stir in flour, salt, white pepper, and nutmeg; cook until bubbling. Remove from heat and gradually mix in half-and-half; cook, stirring, until thick. Boil gently, stirring occasionally, for 2 minutes. Mix in cheese until melted.

Makes about 2½ cups.

Lightly cooked oysters nestle into a bacon-topped frittata to become an Old West favorite: Hangtown Fry.

The recipe for these diminutive
and delicate Swedish Pancakes is
on page 83. There is a feature
on specialty pans, including
this one, on page 85.

Pancakes & Waffles

The very phrase "hot off the griddle" suggests irresistible freshness. Perhaps that is why pancakes, waffles, or French toast mean "Sunday morning" in many homes. For a change in routine, try similar creations from other cultures—crêpes, blintzes, or blini—that are also popular for breakfasts and brunches. All contain some flour, and many are classified as quick breads. Variations such as crêpes and billowy oven pancakes are also very eggy, giving them a certain delicacy. Many of these pancakelike breakfast treats require a special pan or iron to give them a distinctive shape or imprint.

Take a basket full of Blueberry Yogurt Pancakes with butter and warm syrup out onto the patio for breakfast, and get your day off to a delightful start.

If you purchase a new pancake griddle, season it with oil before using. The procedure is the same as seasoning an omelet pan (see page 85). As with an omelet pan, a well-seasoned pancake griddle should not be washed after using. Wipe away any clinging bits with a little oil and a paper towel, and store the griddle in a dry place.

BLUEBERRY YOGURT PANCAKES

These puffy hotcakes are made with a combination of plain yogurt and milk. They are dotted with fresh or frozen blueberries and are delicious with butter and maple syrup.

  1 *cup flour*
  1 *tablespoon sugar*
  1 *teaspoon baking powder*
  ½ *teaspoon baking soda*
  ¼ *teaspoon salt*
  ⅛ *teaspoon ground nutmeg*
  1 *egg*
  ½ *cup each plain yogurt and milk*
  2 *tablespoons salad oil*
  ¾ *cup fresh or unsweetened frozen blueberries*
    Butter or margarine and maple syrup

1. Stir together flour, sugar, baking powder, soda, salt, and nutmeg. Beat egg with yogurt and milk in a large bowl. Beat in oil, then add flour mixture. Stir just until combined. (Batter can be a little lumpy.)

2. Grease seasoned pancake griddle if necessary, and place over medium heat until a few drops of water dance on the hot griddle. For each pancake, pour a scant ¼ cup batter onto the hot griddle. Sprinkle each pancake with several blueberries.

3. Cook pancakes on first side until they are puffed, full of bubbles, and look dry at edges. Then turn and cook until second side is golden brown. Serve at once with butter and syrup.

Makes about 1 dozen 4-inch pancakes.

PANCAKES

The easy way to make pancakes is from a mix. But if you do, you will miss some of the appealing flavors and textures that can be added only during step-by-step preparation. Actually, pancake batter is quite simple—a mixture of flour with a bit of sugar and leavening added to beaten egg, milk, and a little shortening. For quick breakfasts, you can have the dry ingredients combined, all ready to stir into the egg mixture. Do this while your griddle is heating.

BANANA HOTCAKES WITH HONEY-PECAN BUTTER

Mashed fresh banana makes these special pancakes moist and flavorful. The toasted pecan and honey butter is a delicious flavor complement.

1 cup flour
2 teaspoons baking powder
½ teaspoon salt
⅛ teaspoon ground nutmeg
2 tablespoons sugar
1 egg
1 cup milk
3 tablespoons salad oil
1 cup mashed bananas
2 teaspoons lemon juice

Honey-Pecan Butter

⅓ cup pecans
½ cup butter, softened
¼ cup honey

1. Stir together flour, baking powder, salt, nutmeg, and sugar. Beat egg with milk in a large bowl. Beat in oil, then bananas and lemon juice. Add flour mixture. Stir just until combined. (Batter can be a little lumpy.)

2. Grease seasoned pancake griddle if necessary, and place over medium heat until a few drops of water dance on the hot griddle. For each hotcake, pour a scant ¼ cup batter onto hot griddle.

3. Cook hotcakes on first side until they are puffed, full of bubbles, and look dry at edges. Then turn and cook until second side is golden brown. Serve at once with Honey-Pecan Butter.

Makes sixteen to eighteen 3½-inch hotcakes.

Honey-Pecan Butter Spread pecans in a shallow pan. Toast in a 350° F oven for about 8 minutes; cool. Chop toasted pecans finely. In a medium bowl beat butter until fluffy; beat in honey until well combined. Then mix in chopped pecans. If made ahead, cover and refrigerate. Let stand at room temperature to soften before serving.

Makes about 1 cup.

SWEDISH PANCAKES

These small, moist, and delicate pancakes are a specialty of Little River Inn, a welcoming hostelry on the northern California coast near Mendocino. Serve them in the Swedish manner, with butter and lingonberry preserves—or with your favorite syrup. The pancakes require a special pan, described on page 85.

⅔ cup flour
½ teaspoon baking powder
⅛ teaspoon salt
2 eggs, separated
1 cup milk (at room temperature)
¼ cup half-and-half
¼ cup butter or margarine, melted and cooled
   Butter or margarine and lingonberry preserves or syrup

1. Stir together flour, baking powder, and salt. Beat egg yolks with milk and half-and-half in a large bowl. Beat in melted butter, then add flour mixture. Stir to combine.

2. Beat egg whites until stiff but not dry. Fold into batter.

3. Place lightly oiled Swedish pancake pan (see page 85) over medium-low heat until a few drops of water dance on the hot surface. Add about 2 tablespoons of the batter for each pancake. Cook pancakes until golden brown on each side, turning once.

4. Serve hot with butter and preserves or syrup.

Makes twenty-five 3-inch pancakes.

GINGERBREAD PANCAKES WITH LEMON SAUCE

The sauce for these spicy griddlecakes is tart, clear, warm, and lemony. Add homemade sausage patties (see page 67) for a Sunday family breakfast.

1⅓ cups flour
1 teaspoon baking powder
¼ teaspoon each baking soda and salt
½ teaspoon ground ginger
1 teaspoon ground cinnamon
1 egg
1¼ cups milk
¼ cup molasses
3 tablespoons salad oil

Lemon Sauce

½ cup sugar
1 tablespoon cornstarch
   Pinch ground nutmeg
1 cup hot water
2 tablespoons butter or margarine
½ teaspoon grated lemon rind
2 tablespoons lemon juice

1. Stir together flour, baking powder, soda, salt, ginger, and cinnamon. Beat egg with milk in a large bowl. Beat in molasses, then oil. Add flour mixture and stir just until combined. (Batter can be a little lumpy.)

2. Grease seasoned pancake griddle, if necessary, and place over medium heat until a few drops of water dance on the hot griddle. Pour a scant ¼ cup batter onto hot griddle.

3. Cook pancakes on first side until they are puffed, full of bubbles, and look dry at edges. Then turn and cook until second side is browned. Serve with hot Lemon Sauce.

Makes about eighteen 3½-inch pancakes.

Lemon Sauce In a medium saucepan mix sugar, cornstarch, and nutmeg. Gradually mix in water. Cook, stirring, over medium heat until mixture is thick and clear. Add butter, lemon rind, and lemon juice, stirring until butter melts. Serve hot.

Makes about 1⅓ cups.

QUICK BUCKWHEAT BLINI

A yeast-leavened batter gives blini—Russian appetizer pancakes—a tartness that complements the flavor of the buckwheat flour in them.

> *1 package active dry yeast*
> *¼ cup warm water*
> *¾ cup milk*
> *½ teaspoon sugar*
> *¼ teaspoon salt*
> *¼ cup butter, softened*
> *¾ cup all-purpose flour*
> *¼ cup buckwheat flour*
> *1 egg, separated*
> *Melted butter, sour cream, caviar or smoked salmon, and lemon wedges and chopped hard-cooked egg*

1. In large bowl of electric mixer, sprinkle yeast over water. Let stand until softened (about 5 minutes).

2. Heat milk in a medium saucepan until steaming; remove from heat and mix in sugar, salt, and butter, stirring until butter melts. Let stand until cooled to lukewarm. Stir into yeast mixture, then add flours and egg yolk. Mix to blend, then beat until smooth (1 to 2 minutes).

3. Cover bowl and let stand in a warm place until batter is doubled and slightly sour smelling (about 1 hour). Stir batter down. Beat egg white until stiff. Fold egg white into batter. Let stand for 10 minutes.

4. Preheat oven to 250° F. Using 2 to 3 tablespoons batter for each, bake blini in a lightly oiled, preheated 4½- to 5-inch blini pan or in each depression of a Swedish pancake pan (see page 85) until crisp and golden brown on each side. Turn when tops are bubbly and look dry at edges.

5. Keep blini warm in oven until they are all baked, then serve topped with melted butter, sour cream, and caviar or smoked salmon, accompanied by lemon wedges and hard-cooked egg.

Makes 15 to 20 blini.

SPINACH BRUNCH PANCAKES

If you have a Swedish pancake pan, you can also use it to make these diminutive Scandinavian spinach cakes for a brunch. Offer a choice of such toppings as melted butter, sour cream, and red caviar or smoked salmon. As accompaniments, serve a tomato salad with dill dressing and beer or white wine.

> *1½ cups milk*
> *2 eggs*
> *½ teaspoon each salt and sugar*
> *⅛ teaspoon ground nutmeg*
> *1 cup flour*
> *2 tablespoons butter, melted and cooled*
> *1 package (10 oz) frozen chopped spinach, thawed, well drained, and squeezed dry*
> *Butter or margarine*
> *Melted butter, sour cream, and red caviar or smoked salmon*

1. Preheat oven to 250° F. In food processor using plastic blade (or in mixing bowl) combine milk, eggs, salt, sugar, nutmeg, and flour. Process (or beat in bowl) until smooth, stopping motor once or twice to scrape flour from sides of container.

2. Add melted butter and spinach; process (or stir) until well combined.

3. For each pancake, melt a little butter in a 4½- to 5-inch blini pan or in each depression of a Swedish pancake pan (see page 15) over medium heat until bubbling. Add about 2 tablespoons of the spinach batter for each pancake, spreading to cover pan bottom (or individual depressions of Swedish pancake pan). Cook pancakes until lightly browned on each side, turning once. Add a bit more butter for later pancakes.

4. Keep baked pancakes warm on a heatproof serving platter in oven. Serve topped with melted butter, sour cream, and red caviar or smoked salmon.

Makes 20 to 24 pancakes.

CRÊPES

In their country of origin, France, crêpes are served as a snack, a lunch or supper dish, or—depending on flavoring and embellishment—dessert. But that is no reason not to enjoy them for breakfast and brunch.

Filled and sauced in a variety of ways, then baked just before serving, crêpes are the ideal main dish to prepare in advance for a friendly get-together.

You can make basic crêpes that serve well for most main dishes, or sweeten them slightly for dessert. Variations such as main-dish crêpes made with whole wheat or buckwheat flour or with cornmeal, are also possible.

BASIC CRÊPES

Here is the recipe for the plain main-dish crêpes used in several of the recipes that follow. If you wish, they can be made ahead and frozen, then thawed and filled later.

> *1 cup flour*
> *¾ cup water*
> *⅔ cup milk*
> *3 eggs*
> *2 tablespoons salad oil*
> *¼ teaspoon salt*

1. In blender or food processor, combine all ingredients. Whirl or process until batter is smooth, stopping motor once or twice to scrape flour from sides of container.

2. Cover and refrigerate batter for at least 1 hour. Blend batter well before making crêpes.

3. Make crêpes (see page 87) using a lightly oiled 6-inch pan. Stack them as each crêpe is completed.

Makes 16 to 20 crêpes.

SPECIAL PANS FOR SPECIAL PANCAKES

Some of the more fascinating utensils in the cookware world are designed to produce uncommon pancakes and waffles. Some are handsome enough to adorn a kitchen wall. If you enjoy varying your breakfast and brunch repertoire, you will probably want to purchase one or more of these.

The first to consider is a *crêpe pan*. It resembles an omelet pan in that it is fashioned of rolled steel. It differs in one important respect—the crêpe pan has a flat, well-defined bottom (to give the crêpe a sharp edge) and flaring sides. The sides of an omelet pan, on the other hand, curve gently into the bottom.

Season a new crêpe pan as you would an omelet pan (see page 8). Reserve it strictly for crêpes and you will never need to wash it. Just use a paper towel dipped in a little oil to wipe away any crumbs after each use, then store the pan in a dry place to prevent rust. Rub a little oil over the sides and bottom as it heats before

you make the next batch of crêpes.

Crêpe pans range in size from about 5 to 8½ inches (diameter of the crêpe or pan bottom, not the top edge). Most of the crêpe recipes in this book specify 6- to 7-inch crêpes.

A *Breton crêpe griddle* is notable for its larger size—11 to 15 inches in diameter. It is not as deep as smaller crêpe pans, and has just a shallow, upturned rim to contain the crêpe batter. Made of cast aluminum or cast iron, it also can be used as a griddle for modest domestic pancakes, and grilled sandwiches.

A *blini pan*, by contrast, is so small some people mistake it for a one-egg frying pan. It has a bottom diameter of 3½ to 4 inches to shape the diminutive Russian pancakes. Otherwise, it is like a standard crêpe pan in design and should be seasoned and cared for in the same way.

A *Swedish pancake pan*, made for the delicate, eggy pancakes for which a recipe is given on page 83, can also be used to make blini. In one respect it is even more convenient, because you can make several pancakes at a time. The pan is a large (about 10 inches in diameter) cast iron griddle containing 7 shallow, 3-inch-round depressions. Season and treat it as

you would any other cast iron pan (see page 9).

Another attractive Scandinavian utensil is the *heart-shaped waffle iron*. Circular, its cast iron grids consist of five interlocking hearts. Range-top irons must be turned once as the waffles bake.

From France or Belgium comes the inspiration for the cast aluminum *Belgian waffle iron*. (Some are imported and others are made in the United States.) You can find them both plain and with nonstick coatings. They differ from conventional irons in gridding a waffle with deeper pockets to hold more topping.

Also from France is the *croque monsieur iron*, a cast aluminum sandwich grill. It toasts your breakfast sandwich while imprinting it with a cockleshell pattern. With it, even jelly sandwiches look elegant.

The last two, as well as crêpe pans, can be ordered from: Williams-Sonoma, Mail Order Department, Box 3792, San Francisco, CA 94119.

All are available as range-top utensils, and can be used on both gas and electric burners. More sophisticated electric versions of some are made, but this isn't really necessary.

85

CHICKEN AND SPICED APPLE CRÊPES

For brunch, try this subtly sweet crêpe combination with whole green beans and a dry Gewürztraminer.

  5 *tablespoons butter*
  2 *medium-sized tart cooking apples, peeled and coarsely shredded*
  1 *teaspoon each sugar and lemon juice*
  ¼ *teaspoon ground cinnamon*
  ⅛ *teaspoon each ground coriander and ground nutmeg*
  3 *tablespoons flour*
  ¼ *teaspoon salt*
    Dash white pepper
  ¾ *cup chicken broth (from Simmered Chicken)*
  1 *cup half-and-half*
  1 *egg yolk*
 16 *Basic Crêpes, 6 to 7 inches in diameter*
  1 *tablespoon dry white wine*
  ¼ *cup sliced almonds*

Simmered Chicken

  1 *frying chicken (3 to 3½ lbs)*
  ½ *teaspoon salt*
  ⅛ *teaspoon dried thyme*
  ⅛ *teaspoon whole peppercorns (white or black)*
  3 *sprigs parsley*
  1 *stalk celery (chopped)*
  3 *cups water*

1. Preheat oven to 425° F. In a medium frying pan over moderate heat, melt 2 tablespoons of the butter. Stir in apples and cook until just tender, stirring often. Mix in sugar, lemon juice, cinnamon, coriander, and nutmeg. Fold in chicken and set aside.

2. In a medium saucepan over moderate heat, melt remaining 3 tablespoons butter. Stir in flour, salt, and white pepper; cook until bubbling. Remove from heat and gradually blend in chicken broth and half-and-half. Cook, stirring constantly, until thickened. Beat egg yolk in a small bowl; blend in a little of the hot

sauce, then blend mixture, off heat, into remaining sauce. Cook, stirring, over low heat, just until thickened (1 to 2 minutes). Fold about a third of the sauce into chicken-apple mixture.

3. Fill crêpes, dividing chicken mixture evenly, and roll them up. Place side by side in a shallow, buttered 9- by 13-inch baking dish

4. Blend wine into remaining sauce; pour evenly over crêpes. Sprinkle with almonds.

5. Bake until crêpes are heated through and sauce is lightly browned (12 to 15 minutes).

Serves 8.

Simmered Chicken Cut up chicken. Place pieces in a 4½- to 5-quart Dutch oven or deep frying pan. Sprinkle salt, thyme, whole peppers, and parsley over chicken. Add celery and water. Bring to a boil over medium heat. Cover, reduce heat, and simmer just until chicken is tender (40 to 45 minutes). Remove chicken from broth, reserving broth. (Strain, reserving ¾ cup for sauce, and freeze remainder for soups or sauces.) Remove and discard bones and skin. Dice chicken into bite-sized pieces.

Makes 3 to 3½ cups.

MEXICAN CHICKEN AND CHILE CRÊPES

Derived from creamy Mexican *enchiladas Suizas*, this dish is made with crêpes containing just enough cornmeal to give them a slight crunch.

  1 *chicken (3 to 3½ lbs), cut up*
  2 *large tomatoes, peeled and chopped*
  ½ *cup water*
  1 *medium onion, finely chopped*
  1 *clove garlic, minced or pressed*
  1 *teaspoon salt*
  ¼ *teaspoon each ground cumin and ground coriander*
  1 *cup whipping cream*
  1 *can (4 oz) whole green chiles, seeded and chopped*

  2 *cups grated Monterey jack cheese*
  ½ *cup sour cream, mixed until smooth with 2 tablespoons half-and-half*
  ¼ *cup sliced ripe olives*
  3 *green onions, thinly sliced (use part of tops)*

Cornmeal Crêpes

  ¾ *cup flour*
  ¼ *cup yellow cornmeal*
  ¾ *cup water*
  ⅔ *cup milk*
  3 *eggs*
  2 *tablespoons salad oil*
  ¼ *teaspoon salt*

1. Place chicken pieces in a single layer in a large frying pan. Add tomatoes, water, onion, garlic, salt, cumin, and coriander. Bring to a boil over medium heat, cover, reduce heat, and simmer until chicken is very tender (about 1½ hours).

2. Remove chicken pieces from cooking liquid. Remove and discard bones and skin. Shred chicken into bite-sized pieces.

3. Bring cooking liquid to a boil and boil, stirring occasionally, until sauce is thickened and reduced to about 1½ cups. Add cream, then boil again until reduced to about 2 cups. Blend in green chiles. Spread half the sauce in a shallow, buttered baking dish about 9 by 13 inches.

4. Place an equal portion of chicken at end of each crêpe. Roll each crêpe and place side by side in sauce in baking dish. Spoon remaining sauce over crêpes. Sprinkle evenly with cheese. (If made ahead, cover and refrigerate.)

5. Preheat oven to 375° F. Bake, uncovered, for 20 to 30 minutes, until filling is heated through and cheese melts and browns lightly. Spoon sour cream mixture down centers. Sprinkle with olives and green onions.

Serves 8.

Cornmeal Crêpes In blender or food processor, combine flour, cornmeal, water, milk, eggs, oil, and salt. Whirl or process until batter is smooth, stopping motor once or twice to scrape flour down from sides of container. Cover and refrigerate batter for at least 1 hour. Blend batter well before making crêpes. Then make crêpes, using an oiled 6- to 7-inch pan.

Makes 16 to 20 crêpes.

MOUSSAKA-STYLE LAMB CRÊPES

Moussaka is a Greek dish combining layers of lamb and eggplant with a custardy topping. In this variation, whole wheat crêpes replace the eggplant.

- 1 tablespoon olive oil
- 1½ pounds ground lamb, crumbled
- 2 medium onions, finely chopped
- 1 clove garlic, minced or pressed (optional)
- ¾ teaspoon ground cinnamon
- 1 teaspoon salt
- ⅛ teaspoon each ground nutmeg and white pepper
- ¼ teaspoon dried oregano
- ⅓ cup chopped parsley
- 1 can (8 oz) tomato sauce
- ⅔ cup grated Parmesan cheese

Whole Wheat Crêpes

- ¾ cup all-purpose flour
- ¼ cup whole wheat flour
- ¾ cup water
- ⅔ cup milk
- 3 eggs
- 2 tablespoons olive oil or salad oil
- ¼ teaspoon salt

Custard Sauce

- 2 tablespoons butter or margarine
- 2 tablespoons flour
- ½ teaspoon salt
  Dash each ground nutmeg and white pepper
- 2 cups milk
- 2 eggs and 1 egg yolk

1. In a large frying pan over moderately high heat, heat olive oil and cook lamb, stirring until browned. If necessary, spoon off excess fat. Mix in onions and cook, stirring occasionally, until onions are tender. Mix in garlic (if used), cinnamon, salt, nutmeg, white pepper, oregano, parsley, and tomato sauce. Bring to a boil, cover, reduce heat, and simmer for 15 minutes.

2. Remove meat mixture from heat and stir in ⅓ cup cheese.

3. Place an equal portion of filling at end of each crêpe. Roll each crêpe and place side by side in a shallow, buttered baking dish about 9 by 13 inches.

4. Pour sauce evenly over crêpes. Sprinkle evenly with remaining ⅓ cup cheese. (If made ahead, cover and refrigerate.)

5. Preheat oven to 350° F. Bake, uncovered, until top browns lightly (45 minutes to 1 hour).

Serves 8.

Whole Wheat Crêpes In blender or food processor, combine flours, water, milk, eggs, oil, and salt. Whirl or process until batter is smooth, stopping motor once or twice to scrape flour down from sides of container. Cover and refrigerate batter for at least 1 hour. Blend batter well. Then make crêpes, using an oiled 6- to 7-inch pan. Stack as crêpes are completed.

Makes 16 to 20 crêpes.

Custard Sauce Melt butter in a heavy, medium-sized saucepan over moderate heat; stir in flour, salt, nutmeg, and white pepper. Remove from heat and gradually stir in milk. Cook, stirring, until thickened and bubbling. In a medium bowl beat eggs and egg yolk. Mix in a little of the hot sauce. Off heat, blend egg mixture gradually into remaining sauce, over low heat. (Do not boil.)

MAKING AND FILLING CREPES

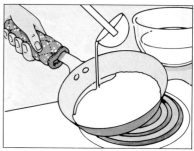

1. *Tilting and swirling the hot pan as you add batter, use just enough to cover the bottom with a thin layer.*

2. *Turn crêpes when the surface looks dry and the underside is golden brown. Use a small spatula to loosen the crêpe; turn with spatula or your fingers. Stack as they are completed.*

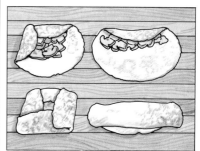

3. *Finished crêpes can be filled as follows: (left) place filling in center, and fold in each edge to make a square with a little filling exposed in center; for rolled crêpes, place filling in a line near edge closest to you, then roll up. Crêpes for blintzes (not shown) are browned on one side only. Place filling in center of browned side, then fold in edges envelope style. Sprinkle filling for a dessert crêpe over half; fold in half lengthwise, then fold in half again to make quarters.*

BRETON SEAFOOD CRÊPES

Filled with flakes of steamed fish and tiny shrimp, these buckwheat-flavored crêpes are covered with a subtle cheese sauce.

   1 pound rock cod or sea
      bass fillets
   3 green onions, thinly sliced
      (use part of tops)
   2 cups grated Gruyère or
      Swiss cheese
   ½ pound tiny peeled, cooked
      shrimp
   2 tablespoons each butter or
      margarine and flour
      Pinch each white pepper,
      ground nutmeg, and
      cayenne pepper
   1 cup milk
   ½ cup chicken broth,
      homemade or canned
   1 tablespoon dry vermouth
   ½ cup grated Parmesan cheese

Buckwheat Crêpes

   ¾ cup plus 2 tablespoons
      all-purpose flour
   2 tablespoons buckwheat flour
   ¾ cup water
   ⅔ cup milk
   3 eggs
   2 tablespoons salad oil
   ¼ teaspoon salt

1. Place fish fillets on a rack above about ½ inch of water in a medium frying pan. Bring water to a boil, cover, reduce heat, and steam until fish looks opaque and flakes when tested with a fork (6 to 8 minutes). Drain and cool, then remove and discard bones and skin, if any. Separate fish into flakes. (You should have about 2 cups.)

2. *To prepare filling:* Mix flaked fish, green onions, 1 cup of the Gruyère cheese, and about half of the shrimp. Fill crêpes, dividing seafood mixture evenly, and roll them up. Place side by side in a shallow, buttered baking dish about 9 by 13 inches.

3. *To prepare sauce:* Melt butter in a 1½-quart saucepan over medium heat. Stir in flour, white pepper, nutmeg, and cayenne; cook until bubbling. Remove from heat and gradually mix in milk and chicken broth. Cook, stirring constantly, until thickened and bubbling. Stir in remaining 1 cup Gruyère cheese until melted; fold in remaining shrimp and vermouth. Pour cheese and shrimp sauce over crêpes; sprinkle with Parmesan cheese.

4. Preheat oven to 400° F. Bake, uncovered, until crêpes are heated through and cheese sauce is lightly browned (20 to 30 minutes).

Serves 8.

Buckwheat Crêpes In blender or food processor combine all-purpose flour, buckwheat flour, water, milk, eggs, oil, and salt. Whirl or process for about 1 minute at high speed; scrape down any flour clinging to sides, then whirl or process again briefly. Cover and refrigerate batter at least 1 hour. Make 6- to 7-inch crêpes (see page 87), stacking them as each crêpe is completed.

Makes 16 to 20 crêpes.

BRETON-STYLE SAUSAGE AND SPINACH CRÊPES

The typical crêpes of Brittany are almost cartwheel size—as large as 12 to 15 inches in diameter. They are made on a slightly rimmed griddle (see the Special Feature on pans, page 85). Unless you shop abroad, you may find the authentic article hard to obtain. You can make the giant crêpes using a pancake griddle (with a bit of a rim, to contain the fluid batter) or a shallow frying pan.

These crêpes are also put together differently from the preceding ones. You place a hot crêpe flat on a big plate, add the filling in the center, then fold in the four sides of the crêpe toward the center to make a plump square. French cider is the beverage of choice in a true crêperie.

   8 Buckwheat Crêpes
      (recipe at left)
   1 pound Polish sausages or
      other smoked garlic sausages
   1 medium onion, finely
      choppped
   ¼ cup butter or margarine
   2 packages (10 oz each) frozen
      chopped spinach, thawed
      and well drained
   1 teaspoon flour
   ½ cup whipping cream
   ¾ teaspoon salt
   ⅛ teaspoon each ground nutmeg
      and white pepper

1. Prepare batter for crêpes and let stand as directed. Make 10- to 12-inch crêpes, using a large Breton crêpe pan or a pancake griddle, stacking them as each crêpe is completed. If made ahead, place in a buttered shallow pan, cover lightly with foil, and reheat in a 250° F oven until crêpes are warmed through (about 15 minutes).

2. Pierce sausages in several places with a fork. Place in a deep frying pan, pour on water to cover, and bring slowly to just under the boiling point; cover, reduce heat, and simmer very slowly for 20 minutes.

3. In a large frying pan, cook onion in 2 tablespoons of the butter over medium heat until soft. Mix in spinach, flour, cream, salt, nutmeg, and white pepper. Cook, stirring often, until mixture is thick and bubbling.

4. Drain sausages and slice on the diagonal about ¼ inch thick. In a large frying pan over moderately high heat, melt remaining 2 tablespoons butter and cook sausage slices, turning often, until lightly browned.

5. To assemble, place a warm crêpe on a warm plate, and spoon a dollop of spinach mixture in center. Add several browned sausage slices. Fold in edges of crêpe toward center to make a square.

Serves 8.

Sausage
Spinach
Crêpes
Orange
Crêpes
French Cider
Café

Flaming Orange-Buttered Dessert Crêpes (page 92) cap an all-crêpe brunch menu that begins with oversized Breton-Style Sausage and Spinach Crêpes.

The recipe continues with ingredients listed at top right:

16 Basic Crêpes, 6 to 7 inches
   in diameter (see page 84)
 3 tablespoons flour
 1 teaspoon Dijon mustard
   Dash cayenne pepper
1½ cups half-and-half
 ¼ cup dry white wine
 ⅓ cup grated Parmesan cheese

1. In a large frying pan over medium-high heat, melt 3 tablespoons of the butter. Cook and stir asparagus, green onions, and mushrooms until mushrooms brown lightly and any liquid is gone. Mix in lemon juice, ½ teaspoon of the salt, tarragon, and white pepper. Remove from heat and mix in ½ cup of the Gruyère cheese.

2. Fill crêpes, dividing vegetable mixture evenly, and roll them up. Place side by side in a shallow, buttered baking dish about 9 by 13 inches.

3. For sauce, melt remaining 3 tablespoons butter in a 2-quart saucepan, then stir in flour and cook until bubbly. Add remaining ½ teaspoon salt, mustard, and cayenne. Remove from heat and gradually blend in half-and-half, then wine. Return to heat and cook, stirring constantly, until thick. Stir in ½ cup more Gruyère cheese until melted.

4. Pour sauce over crêpes. Sprinkle evenly with remaining 1 cup Gruyère cheese and Parmesan cheese. (If made ahead, cover and refrigerate.)

5. Preheat oven to 400° F. Bake, uncovered, until crêpes are heated through and lightly browned (30 to 35 minutes; about 45 minutes if refrigerated).

Serves 6 to 8.

An appetizing variety of fresh foods come together tastefully in Asparagus and Mushroom Crêpes. A white wine, such as Chenin Blanc, and a mixed-fruit salad are complementary.

ASPARAGUS AND MUSHROOM CRÊPES

Here is a tantalizing way to make a small amount of fresh asparagus serve at least 6 people—combine it with mushrooms and a cheese sauce in rolled crêpes.

 6 tablespoons butter or
   margarine
 3 cups cut asparagus (diagonal
   ½-in. lengths)
 4 green onions, thinly sliced
 ½ pound mushrooms, sliced
 1 teaspoon each lemon juice
   and salt
 ¼ teaspoon dried tarragon
   Dash white pepper
 2 cups grated Gruyère or Swiss
   cheese

TRUFFLED HAM AND CHEESE CRÊPES

It isn't absolutely necessary to include the costly truffle in these baked crêpes, but it is an elegant and impressive addition. A full-bodied dry rosé wine or a *blanc de noir* such as a "white" Zinfandel or blanc de Pinot Noir pairs well with the crêpes.

> 2 tablespoons butter
> ¼ cup finely chopped shallots or mild onion
> 1 egg
> ¼ cup soft bread crumbs
> 3 cups ground cooked smoked ham
> 2 cups grated Gruyère or Swiss cheese
> 1 or 2 black truffles (optional)
> 16 Basic Crêpes, 6 to 7 inches in diameter (see page 84)

Wine-Cream Sauce

> 2 tablespoons butter
> 2 tablespoons flour
> ¼ teaspoon each salt and dry mustard
> Pinch cayenne pepper
> 1½ cups half-and-half
> ¼ cup dry white wine
> 1 egg yolk
> ¼ cup grated Parmesan cheese

1. In a small frying pan, melt butter and cook shallots until soft and lightly browned; remove from heat.

2. In a medium bowl beat egg lightly; blend in bread crumbs and shallot mixture. Then add ham and 1 cup of the cheese. Slice truffles (if used) very thinly; reserve half the slices for topping. Sliver remaining slices and add to ham mixture. If using canned truffles, add any liquid to filling.

3. Place an equal portion of filling at end of each crêpe. Roll each crêpe and place side by side in a shallow, buttered 9- by 13-inch baking dish.

4. Pour Wine-Cream Sauce evenly over crêpes. Scatter remaining truffle slices over sauce. Sprinkle evenly with remaining 1 cup cheese. (If made ahead, cover and refrigerate.)

5. Preheat oven to 400° F. Bake, uncovered, until crêpes are heated through and lightly browned (25 to 30 minutes; about 35 minutes if refrigerated).

Serves 8.

Wine-Cream Sauce Melt butter in a medium-sized, heavy saucepan. Stir in flour and cook until bubbly. Mix in salt, dry mustard, and cayenne. Remove from heat; gradually blend in half-and-half, then wine. Return to heat and cook, stirring constantly, until thickened and bubbling. In a small bowl beat egg yolk; gradually blend in a little of the hot sauce. Stir into remaining sauce off heat; return to low heat. Cook and stir until thick. (Do not boil.) Mix in cheese.

Makes about 2 cups.

SAVORY TURKEY CRÊPES

Reminiscent of canneloni, these crêpes are stuffed with uncooked ground turkey. Therefore, they require a longer baking time than other filled crêpes that need only to be heated through. Accompany the dish with a green salad or cooked green vegetable and a light red wine such as a young Beaujolais or a Gamay from the Loire Valley of France.

> ¼ cup butter or margarine
> 1 medium onion, finely chopped
> 1 egg
> ½ cup each sour cream and soft bread crumbs
> 1 teaspoon each salt and Dijon mustard
> ⅛ teaspoon each ground nutmeg, dried sage leaves, and white pepper
> 2 pounds ground turkey
> 16 Basic Crêpes, 6 to 7 inches in diameter (see page 84)
> 2 tablespoons flour
> Pinch cayenne pepper
> 1 cup milk
> ½ cup canned tomato sauce
> 2 tablespoons each dry vermouth and chopped parsley
> 1½ cups grated Gruyère or Swiss cheese

1. Preheat oven to 375° F. In a small frying pan, melt 2 tablespoons of the butter and cook onion until soft and lightly browned. In a large bowl beat egg with sour cream. Mix in bread crumbs, salt, mustard, nutmeg, sage, and white pepper. Then lightly mix in turkey and cooked onion.

2. Fill crêpes with turkey mixture. Roll up and place side by side in a buttered 9- by 13-inch baking dish.

3. For sauce, melt remaining 2 tablespoons butter in a medium saucepan. Stir in flour and cayenne; cook until bubbling. Remove from heat and gradually mix in milk, then tomato sauce (adding it about 2 tablespoons at a time). Cook, stirring, until thickened and bubbling. Remove from heat and mix in vermouth and parsley.

4. Pour tomato sauce evenly over crêpes; sprinkle with grated cheese.

5. Bake, uncovered, until turkey filling is cooked through and cheese browns lightly (1 to 1¼ hours).

Serves 6 to 8.

ORANGE-BUTTERED DESSERT CRÊPES

If you would like your brunch menu to resemble that of a French crêperie, then the dessert that follows a crêpe main dish is a sweet crêpe. For this one the crêpes are filled with a fresh orange butter, then flamed with orange-flavored liqueur.

- 1 cup flour
- 2 tablespoons confectioners' sugar
- ¾ cup water
- ⅔ cup milk
- 3 eggs
- 2 tablespoons salad oil
- ½ teaspoon vanilla extract
- ¼ teaspoon salt
- ½ cup orange-flavored liqueur or *whipped cream to taste*

Orange Butter

- ½ cup butter, softened
- ½ cup sugar
- Grated rind of 1 orange
- 3 tablespoons orange juice

1. In blender or food processor combine flour, confectioners' sugar, water, milk, eggs, oil, vanilla, and salt. Whirl or process until batter is smooth, stopping motor once or twice to scrape flour from sides of container. Cover and refrigerate batter for at least 1 hour.

2. Blend batter well before making crêpes, then make crêpes using a lightly oiled 6- to 7-inch pan (see page 88). Stack them as each crêpe is completed. If made ahead, place in a shallow pan, cover lightly with foil, and reheat in a 250° F oven until crêpes are warmed through (about 15 minutes).

3. To serve, spoon some of the Orange Butter onto half of each crêpe, using a scant tablespoon for each; fold crêpes in quarters, and arrange, slightly overlapping, on a warm, rimmed, heatproof platter.

4. If you wish, flame the crêpes by heating orange-flavored liqueur in a small metal pan until barely warm to touch. (Liqueur will not flame if overheated.) Ignite carefully and pour, flaming, over crêpes. Lift crêpes with 2 forks until flames die out. Serve at once on warm plates. If you do not flame the crêpes, serve crêpes with whipped cream.

Serves 6.

Orange Butter In a medium bowl beat butter until fluffy. Gradually beat in sugar, then blend in orange rind. Adding about 2 teaspoons at a time, gradually beat in orange juice. (If made ahead, cover and refrigerate; let stand at room temperature at least 1 hour before serving.)

Makes about 1 cup.

ALMOND DESSERT CRÊPES

Amaretto liqueur glamorizes the filling of these almond-sprinkled baked dessert crêpes.

- 18 to 20 crêpes from Orange-Buttered Dessert Crêpes, at left
- ⅓ cup butter or margarine, softened
- ⅔ cup sugar
- ½ teaspoon each *grated lemon rind and almond extract*
- 1 egg
- 1 tablespoon almond-flavored liqueur
- ¼ cup flour
- 1 cup ground blanched almonds (whirled in blender or food processor until powdery)
- 2 tablespoons butter or margarine
- ¼ cup sliced almonds
- Whipped cream

1. Make crêpes as directed in steps 1 and 2 of recipe at left; set aside while preparing filling.

2. In a medium bowl beat the ⅓ cup butter until fluffy. Gradually beat in sugar, then blend in lemon rind and almond extract. Beat in egg until smoothly blended. Mix in liqueur, then flour and ground almonds. Beat until well combined.

3. Preheat oven to 425° F. Place an equal portion of almond filling at end of each crêpe. Roll each crêpe and place side by side in a shallow, buttered baking dish about 9 by 13 inches. Dot with the 2 tablespoons butter, then sprinkle with sliced almonds.

4. Bake until crêpes are hot and edges are crisp (10 to 12 minutes). Serve hot with whipped cream.

Serves 6 to 8.

BUTTERMILK BLINTZES

Blintzes aren't crêpes, but you can make these thin pancakes in a crêpe pan. The difference in technique is that at first the blintzes are browned on only one side. After they have been wrapped around a distinctive cheese filling, the blintzes are then fried to brown the other side.

Making blintzes is a lengthy operation. If you make them ahead, you can cover and refrigerate the filled blintzes for up to 24 hours. Then brown quickly and serve hot.

- ¾ cup flour
- ¾ teaspoon baking soda
- ½ teaspoon salt
- 2 tablespoons sugar
- 1 cup buttermilk
- ½ cup water
- 3 eggs
- 2 tablespoons vegetable oil
- 3 to 4 tablespoons each *butter or margarine and vegetable oil, for frying*
- Sour cream
- Cherry preserves

Cheese Filling

- 1 package (8 oz) cream cheese, softened
- 1 egg
- 2 tablespoons confectioners' sugar
- ½ teaspoon vanilla extract
- ¼ teaspoon ground cinnamon
- 2 cups (1 pound) pot cheese (also called farmer's cheese)

1. In blender or food processor, combine flour, soda, salt, sugar, buttermilk, water, eggs, and oil. Whirl or process until batter is smooth, stopping motor once or twice to scrape flour from sides of container. Cover and refrigerate for at least 1 hour before using batter.

2. Make blintzes in a lightly oiled 6- to 7-inch pan as for crêpes, but brown them on first side only and cook until top surface is dry to touch. Stack blintzes to cool.

3. To fill each blintz, place a dollop (about 2 tablespoons) of Cheese Filling in center of browned side of each pancake. Fold in opposite edges about 1 inch, then fold in remaining edges to enclose filling, overlapping in center to make a slightly rectangular-shaped "envelope." Set blintzes aside, folded side down.

4. In a large frying pan over moderately high heat, melt 2 tablespoons of the butter with 2 tablespoons of the oil. Fry filled blintzes without crowding until golden on each side (1 to 1½ minutes on each side). Add more butter and oil to pan as needed.

5. Drain blintzes and serve on warm plates, topped with sour cream and preserves.

Makes 20 to 24 blintzes.

Cheese Filling In a large bowl beat cream cheese with egg, confectioners' sugar, vanilla, and cinnamon. Then beat in cheese.

Makes about 3 cups.

Make Buttermilk Blintzes ahead, including the filling and the folding, and refrigerate them. Later, brown the blintzes and serve them hot with sour cream and cherry preserves.

1. In blender or food processor combine eggs, milk, water, flour, and salt; whirl or process, stopping motor to scrape down sides of container once or twice. Refrigerate batter for 1 hour or longer.

2. Preheat oven to 375° F. Pierce each sausage in several places with a fork. In a large frying pan over medium heat, brown slowly on all sides for 8 to 10 minutes. Reserve drippings. Cut sausages into 1½-inch chunks.

3. Place butter in a 9-inch square baking pan, 10-inch quiche dish, or 10-inch pie pan. Heat in oven until butter melts (5 to 8 minutes), add reserved sausage drippings and chunks of sausage. Pour in batter.

4. Bake until pancake is puffy and well browned (30 to 35 minutes). Cut into squares or wedges and serve immediately.

Serves 4 to 6.

Toad-in-the-Hole is a heartier sort of oven pancake, reminiscent of Yorkshire pudding. Studded with sausage chunks, it is good with a green salad and a country-style bread.

OVEN PANCAKES

This popoverlike batter baked in a large round or square pan puffs spectacularly and forms a crisp crust. This sort of oven pancake serves several people easily and invites variations, either as additions to the batter before baking or as toppings afterward.

TOAD-IN-THE-HOLE

This English dish is a lot like Yorkshire pudding, but rather than being served as an accompaniment to roast beef, it is a main dish studded with chunks of sausage. For brunch, add mustard pickles or a green salad with a mustard-flavored vinaigrette and toasted country bread.

> 2 eggs
> ¾ cup milk
> ¼ cup water
> 1 cup flour
> ¼ teaspoon salt
> 1 pound Italian sausages
> ¼ cup butter or margarine

HONEYED OVEN PANCAKE

Summer fruits complement this honey-sweetened oven pancake. Try it with honey-drizzled sliced peaches or nectarines, the Peaches and Blueberries with Cream on page 31 (if you use the cream, whip it until stiff), or sliced strawberries with sour cream and brown sugar.

> 3 tablespoons butter or
>   margarine
> 3 eggs
> 3 tablespoons honey
> ¼ teaspoon salt
> 1¾ cups milk
> ¾ cup flour
>   Fresh fruit topping

1. Place butter in a 10-inch pie pan, 10-inch quiche dish, or 10-inch frying pan with heatproof handle. Place pan in 425° F oven as it preheats; when butter is melted, remove pan from oven. (Don't let butter burn.)

2. While butter is melting, beat eggs with honey, salt, and milk. Then beat in flour until mixture is smooth. Pour batter into melted butter in hot pan.

3. Bake in 425° F oven until pancake is browned, edges are puffed, and a knife inserted in center comes out clean (20 to 25 minutes). Cut in wedges and serve immediately, adding fruit topping at the table.

Serves 3 to 4.

FRENCH TOAST

If you were served French toast in France it would be called *pain perdu* or "lost bread"—yesterday's bread rescued from inedibility by being dipped it in a mixture of egg and milk, and then browned in butter. It is a fine way of making a breakfast specialty with a few ingredients that are usually at hand.

JAM-FILLED FRENCH TOAST

Sourdough bread is a fine flavor foil for the luscious center of preserves in each thick slice of this French toast. Serve more of the same preserves or jam on the side if you wish.

> 8 *slices (each 1½ in. thick) day-old sourdough French bread*
> ½ *cup favorite fruit preserve, jam, or marmalade*
> 2 *eggs*
> 1 *tablespoon granulated sugar*
> ¾ *cup milk*
> ½ *teaspoon vanilla extract*
> ⅛ *teaspoon ground cinnamon*
> 2 *tablespoons butter*
> 1 *tablespoon salad oil*
>   *Confectioners' sugar*

1. Cutting from bottom of each slice through center almost to top, slash a pocket in each piece of bread. Squeeze bread slice lightly to open pocket and fill each pocket with about 1 tablespoon of preserves, jam, or marmalade.

2. In a shallow bowl beat eggs with granulated sugar, milk, vanilla, and cinnamon. Dip each filled bread slice in egg mixture to coat well.

3. In a large, shallow frying pan, melt 1 tablespoon of the butter with oil over medium heat until mixture is foamy. Add bread slices, 4 at a time, and cook until well browned and crisp on each side, turn once, adding remaining butter as needed.

4. Serve French toast hot, sprinkled with confectioners' sugar.

Serves 4.

MONTE CRISTO SANDWICH

A French-toasted ham, cheese, and turkey sandwich makes a stylish brunch dish. The traditional finish for this hot sandwich is a dusting of powdered sugar and a dollop of currant jelly, but you can omit them if you prefer less sweetness.

> 8 *slices white bread, crusts trimmed*
> 8 *thin slices (about 4 oz) Swiss cheese, cut to fit bread*
> 4 *slices (3 oz) baked ham*
> 4 *slices (3 oz) roast turkey breast*
> 2 *eggs*
> ¼ *cup half-and-half*
>   *Pinch each ground nutmeg and white pepper*
> 2 *tablespoons butter or margarine*
>   *Confectioners' sugar and red currant jelly (optional)*

1. Preheat oven to 400° F. To make sandwiches, place on each of 4 slices of the bread, in order: a slice *each* of cheese, ham, turkey, then another slice of cheese. Complete each sandwich with another slice of bread. Cut sandwiches in halves.

2. Beat eggs in a shallow bowl with half-and-half, nutmeg, and white pepper. Dip sandwiches in egg mixture to coat well on both sides.

3. In a large frying pan over medium heat, melt butter; brown sandwiches lightly on both sides, turning once. Place on a baking sheet and bake until cheese melts (3 to 5 minutes).

4. Sprinkle lightly with confectioners' sugar and accompany with currant jelly, if desired. Serve hot.

Makes 4 sandwiches.

GRILLED CHEESE-AND-TOMATO SANDWICHES

The intriguing *croque monsieur* iron—resembling a Belgian waffle iron—gives a shell-like imprint to this toasted sandwich. (Cooks without one of these handy gadgets can use a griddle instead.) See the Special Feature on page 85 for more information on this iron.

> 4 *slices whole wheat, rye, or egg bread*
>   *Mustard (optional)*
> 6 *slices (3 oz) Swiss or Cheddar cheese cut to fit bread*
> 2 *thin slices firm-ripe tomato*
>   *Butter or margarine*

1. Spread 2 of the bread slices lightly with mustard of your choice (if used). (Try coarsely ground or tarragon-flavored Dijon mustard.) Cover each slice with half of the cheese and a tomato slice. Place remaining bread slices over tomatoes to complete sandwiches.

2. Spread tops of sandwiches generously with butter. Place, buttered side down, in seasoned *croque monsieur* toasting iron or on greased griddle. Spread other side of sandwiches generously with butter. If using a *croque monsieur* iron, close it and hook the latch on the handle; if any bread extends beyond edges, trim and discard it.

3. Place iron or griddle over medium heat and cook until well browned on both sides, turning once (4 to 5 minutes on first side, then 2 to 3 minutes on second). Serve at once.

Makes 2 sandwiches.

WAFFLES

The iron in which waffles are baked—and which gives them their distinctive gridlike pattern—may take a round, square, or rectangular shape. Some irons are electric; others are designed for use on top of the range. In any case, the grids of a waffle iron—like a crêpe pan or a pancake griddle—should be seasoned well and then never washed. Season the grids before first use as you would an omelet or crêpe pan (see page 85), or follow the manufacturer's directions for seasoning a waffle iron with a nonstick coating. If you don't use your waffle iron often, brush the grids lightly with salad oil before heating the iron.

SCANDINAVIAN HEART-SHAPED WAFFLES

These unusual sour cream waffles are made in the charming waffle iron shown on page 85. You might make them to serve as part of a Scandinavian breakfast buffet with herring, sliced cold meats, cheese, crisp flatbread, and lots of coffee. The waffles can be made ahead and reheated in a warm oven. They're easiest to eat as a finger food, like cookies.

- *¾ cup flour*
- *2 teaspoons baking powder*
- *2 eggs, separated*
- *1¼ cups sour cream*
- *1 tablespoon salad oil*
  Confectioners' sugar and lingonberry or tart cherry preserves

1. Stir together flour and baking powder. Beat egg yolks with sour cream in a large bowl. Blend in oil. Then add flour mixture and stir just until combined.

2. Beat egg whites until stiff but not dry. Fold into batter.

3. Spoon a generous tablespoon of batter into each section of a heated heart-shaped waffle iron. Bake until golden brown (about 2 minutes on first side and 3 minutes on second).

4. Serve hot, topped with a sprinkling of confectioners' sugar and a dollop of preserves.

Makes 5 waffles.

BELGIAN WAFFLES WITH BLUEBERRY SAUCE

Made from a yeast batter, these waffles with their fresh berry sauce are a summer treat. A special waffle iron, imported from France, gives the deep, rectangular shape (see page 85).

- *1 package active dry yeast*
- *¼ cup warm water*
- *2 cups flour*
- *¼ cup sugar*
- *¼ teaspoon salt*
- *¼ cup butter or margarine, melted and cooled*
- *2 tablespoons salad oil*
- *1½ cups water*
- *½ teaspoon vanilla extract*
- *2 eggs, separated*
  Whipped cream (optional)

Blueberry Sauce

- *⅓ cup butter*
- *⅔ cup sugar*
- *3 tablespoons light corn syrup*
- *¼ cup water*
- *2 tablespoons grated lemon rind*
- *¼ teaspoon ground nutmeg*
- *1½ cups fresh or frozen unsweetened blueberries*

1. Sprinkle yeast over the ¼ cup warm water in a small bowl; let stand about 5 minutes to soften. In a large bowl mix flour, sugar, and salt. Beat in butter, oil, the 1½ cups water, and vanilla until smooth. Then beat in egg yolks and yeast mixture.

2. Beat egg whites until they form soft peaks; fold gently into batter. Cover and refrigerate for several hours or overnight; stir down batter.

3. Place a seasoned 6- by 7½-inch Belgian waffle iron directly over medium heat, turning it over occasionally, until a few drops of water dance on the grids. Spoon about ½ cup batter into the iron, spreading it to just cover grids.

4. Close the iron and turn it occasionally until waffle is well browned (4 to 5 minutes in all). Transfer waffles to a wire rack unless served immediately.

5. If made ahead, cool waffles, wrap in foil, and freeze. Then preheat oven to 325° F. Reheat, uncovered, in a single layer on baking sheets until hot and crisp (about 10 minutes).

6. Serve hot, with hot Blueberry Sauce poured over. Add whipped cream, if desired.

Makes 9 waffles.

Blueberry Sauce Combine butter, sugar, and corn syrup in a medium saucepan. Place over medium heat and cook, stirring, until mixture boils. Mix in water and bring again to a boil; boil for 2 minutes. Add lemon rind, nutmeg, and blueberries. Cook, stirring, until mixture boils.

Makes about 1¾ cups.

SESAME WAFFLES

Sesame seeds add a nutlike flavor to these crisp waffles.

- *1 cup flour*
- *1½ teaspoons baking powder*
- *⅛ teaspoon salt*
- *1 tablespoon sesame seed*
- *2 eggs, separated*
- *¾ cup milk*
- *½ teaspoon vanilla extract*
- *¼ cup butter or margarine, melted and cooled*
  Butter or margarine and maple syrup

1. Stir together flour, baking powder, salt, and sesame seed. Beat egg yolks with milk in a large bowl. Blend in vanilla and melted butter. Then add flour mixture and stir just until combined.

2. Beat egg whites until stiff but not dry. Fold into batter.

3. Spoon batter into center of heated waffle iron, using about a fourth of the batter for each waffle. Bake until steaming stops, about 5 minutes. Remove waffles carefully and serve at once with butter and syrup.

Makes four 7-inch waffles.

PUFFY CORN FRITTERS

Here is another dish that isn't a pancake, crêpe, or waffle. The reason these simple corn fritters appear with these foods is that they share an affinity for maple syrup. You might also serve them, without the syrup, as a vegetable accompaniment to breakfast meats.

⅓ cup flour
½ teaspoon salt
  Pinch ground coriander
2 eggs. separated
1 package (10 oz) frozen
  whole-kernel corn, thawed
  Salad oil, for frying
  Maple syrup (optional)

1. Stir together flour, salt, and coriander. In a large bowl beat egg yolks slightly. Mix in corn. Add flour mixture, mixing until blended.

2. Beat egg whites until stiff but not dry. Fold into corn mixture.

3. Pour oil into a deep, heavy frying pan to a depth of about ¼ inch. Heat over medium heat until a bit of the corn mixture sizzles when dropped into the oil. Drop corn mixture by rounded tablespoons into oil. Cook fritters until golden brown on each side, turning once (3 to 4 minutes in all). Drain well.

4. Serve fritters hot, with syrup, if desired.

Makes 20 fritters.

Menu

BREAKFAST IN BED

*French Toast with
Strawberries*

*Sautéed Canadian-
Style Bacon*

Breakfast Tea

Treat someone to a breakfast in bed of cinnamon-spiced French toast garlanded by sliced fresh strawberries sweetened with fragrant vanilla sugar.

Thinly sliced Canadian-style bacon needs only a brief turning in heated butter in another pan while the French toast is browning and the tea steeps.

FRENCH TOAST WITH STRAWBERRIES

2 cups strawberries
  Vanilla Sugar (see page 30)
3 eggs
2 teaspoons sugar
¼ teaspoon ground cinnamon
½ cup half-and-half
8 slices French bread
¼ to ½ cup butter or margarine
  Sour cream

1. Preheat oven to 250° F. Remove and discard hulls from strawberries; slice and sweeten to taste with some of the Vanilla Sugar. Set aside while preparing French toast.

2. Beat eggs with sugar, cinnamon, and half-and-half in a shallow dish. Dip bread slices in egg mixture to coat well.

3. In a large frying pan over medium heat, melt 2 tablespoons of the butter. Brown bread slices on both sides, adding more butter as needed. Keep French toast warm in oven until all is ready.

4. Serve French toast with strawberries spooned over and a dollop of sour cream on each piece. Serve additional Vanilla Sugar to taste.

Serves 4.

In Ratatouille in a Whole Wheat Shell (page 105), served here with wine and cheese, a honeyed wheat pastry encloses a ratatouille filling.

Breakfast Pies

I f you like pie, you probably can't resist a flaky wedge of it for breakfast—or at least for brunch. The possibilities for enclosing morning foods in crusts are vast. Try cream quiches puffed with eggs, cheese, vegetables, or bits of ham for the classic breakfast pie. Or bring a full-scale late-morning brunch to a memorable conclusion with a generous fresh fruit tart. Bake pies ahead and heat them before breakfast or brunch, or prebake pie shells so they're ready for fresh fillings made in the morning.

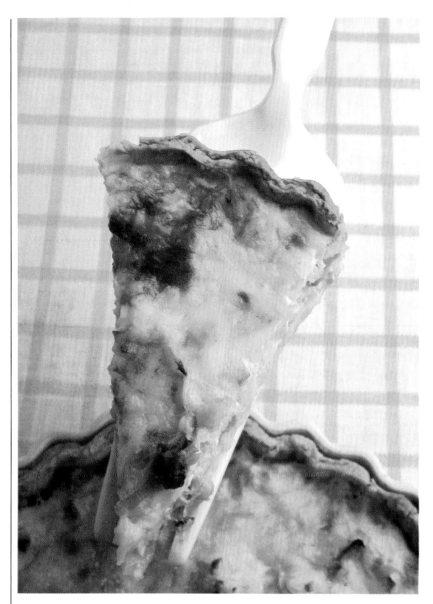

A vegetarian favorite, Leek Quiche is rich with cheese. An egg and butter pastry is the foundation for all the varied and delicious quiches in this chapter.

QUICHES

The pastries involved in breakfast pies take many forms. For a quiche, use an egg-rich flaky pastry, shortened with a combination of butter and lard. A mixture of all-purpose flour and a touch of whole wheat or rye flour or cornmeal will give a quiche crust a flavor and texture boost. Roll the crust slightly thicker than the usual pie crust; this will hold the quiche filling firmly.

EGG PASTRY FOR QUICHE

> 1¼ cups flour
> ¼ teaspoon salt
> ¼ cup butter
> 2 tablespoons lard
> 1 egg, slightly beaten

1. In a medium bowl mix flour and salt. Using a pastry blender or two knives, cut in butter and lard until mixture is crumbly.

2. Gradually add egg to flour mixture, stirring until it is evenly moistened and begins to cling together. Shape into a flattened ball.

3. Roll out on a floured board or pastry cloth to about a 13-inch circle. Fit pastry into a 10-inch quiche dish. Trim edge to about a ½-inch overhang, then fold pastry under, even with top of dish.

4. Fill and bake as directed in the following recipes.

Makes one 10-inch quiche crust.

LEEK QUICHE

Briefly cooked leeks give this meatless quiche a French accent. Serve with baked ham and a lettuce salad.

> 3 large leeks
> 2 tablespoons butter
> Egg Pastry for Quiche, unbaked (recipe above)
> 1¼ cups grated Gruyère or Swiss cheese
> 3 eggs
> 1 cup half-and-half
> 1 teaspoon Dijon mustard
> ½ teaspoon salt
> Pinch each *white pepper and ground nutmeg*

1. Preheat oven to 450° F. Cut off root ends of leeks; remove coarse outer leaves. Cut off upper parts of green tops, leaving about 10-inch-long leeks. Split lengthwise, from stem ends, cutting to within about 1 inch of root ends. Soak in cold water to cover for several minutes; then separate leaves under running water to rinse away any clinging grit; drain well. Slice about ⅛ inch thick.

2. In a large frying pan, melt butter over medium heat. Add sliced leeks; cook, stirring often, until leeks are limp and bright green (6 to 8 minutes). Distribute leeks evenly in Egg Pastry shell. Sprinkle with 1 cup of the cheese.

3. Beat eggs with half-and-half, mustard, salt, white pepper, and nutmeg; pour over cheese.

4. Bake quiche for 10 minutes; reduce heat to 350° F and continue baking for 15 minutes longer. Sprinkle quiche evenly with remaining ¼ cup cheese, then bake until crust is nicely browned and filling is just set in center (5 to 10 minutes more).

5. Let stand about 3 minutes before cutting in wedges to serve.

Serves 6.

ASPARAGUS AND SEAFOOD QUICHE

Either crab or tiny shrimp complement the spokes of fresh asparagus in this handsome quiche. For brunch serve a Chardonnay or Fumé Blanc wine with the pie.

> 6 to 8 asparagus spears (about ¾ lb)
> 2 tablespoons butter or margarine
> ¼ cup finely chopped shallots or mild onion
> ½ pound cooked crab, flaked, or tiny peeled, cooked shrimp Pinch white pepper
> ¼ cup chopped parsley Egg Pastry for Quiche, unbaked (see page 100)
> 1 cup grated Swiss cheese
> 4 eggs
> 1⅓ cups half-and-half
> ½ teaspoon salt
> 1 teaspoon Dijon mustard
> ¼ teaspoon paprika

1. Preheat oven to 450° F. Snap off fibrous ends of asparagus spears; cook, uncovered, in a small amount of boiling salted water in a wide frying pan just until bright green and barely crisp-tender (3 to 4 minutes). Drain and reserve.

2. In a medium frying pan, melt butter and cook shallots until soft but not brown; remove from heat and lightly mix in crab or shrimp, white pepper, and parsley. Distribute shellfish mixture evenly in Egg Pastry shell. Sprinkle with cheese, then arrange asparagus spears, like spokes, over it.

3. Beat eggs with half-and-half, salt, mustard, and paprika; pour over asparagus.

4. Bake quiche for 10 minutes; reduce heat to 350° F and continue baking until crust is well browned and filling is set in center (20 to 25 minutes longer).

5. Let stand about 3 minutes before cutting in wedges to serve.

Serves 6 to 8.

Asparagus spears radiate from the center of Asparagus and Seafood Quiche. Tiny shrimp are hidden in the filling.

Cornmeal-accented pastry cloaks chicken, ham, mushrooms, and peas in a traditional favorite, Chicken Pot Pie.

CHICKEN POT PIE

Made in every respect from scratch, this traditional chicken pie is a bit of a chore. However, it can be assembled in advance and refrigerated.

- ¼ cup butter or margarine
- 1 small onion, finely chopped
- ¼ pound mushrooms, thinly sliced
- 2 tablespoons flour
  Dash each *white pepper* and *nutmeg*
- ½ cup julienned ham
- ½ cup frozen peas, thawed

Simmered Chicken and Broth

- 1 large frying chicken (3½ to 4 lbs)
- 1 small onion, coarsely chopped
- 1 medium carrot, cut into ½-inch slices
- 2 sprigs parsley
- ½ bay leaf
- 1 celery stalk, coarsely chopped
- 1 teaspoon salt
- ¼ teaspoon dried thyme
- 3 cups water

Cornmeal Pastry

- 1 cup flour
- ¼ cup yellow cornmeal
- ¼ teaspoon salt
- ¼ cup cold butter or margarine
- 2 tablespoons lard or soft shortening
- 1 egg yolk
- 2 tablespoons cold water

1. Prepare Simmered Chicken and Broth as directed.

2. Preheat oven to 425° F. In a large, heavy saucepan over medium heat, melt butter. In it cook onion and mushrooms until mushrooms brown lightly. Stir in flour, white pepper, and nutmeg, cooking until bubbly. Remove from heat and gradually stir in the 1½ cups reserved chicken broth. Return to heat and cook, stirring, until mixture is thickened.

3. Mix in chicken pieces, ham strips, and peas. Taste, and add salt if needed. Spread chicken mixture in a 10-inch quiche dish or a 10-inch pie plate. Place Cornmeal Pastry over chicken mixture; trim edge so that it extends about ¾ inch beyond edge of baking dish. Fold pastry edge under, flush with edge of dish; press firmly against edge of quiche dish, or flute edge if using a pie plate. Cut slits in top for steam to escape.

4. Beat egg white reserved from pastry with 1 teaspoon water. Brush over top of crust. Bake until pastry is well browned and filling bubbles (25 to 30 minutes).

Serves 6.

Simmered Chicken and Broth

Cut chicken into serving pieces. In a 4- to 5-quart kettle or Dutch oven, combine chicken pieces, onion, carrot, parsley, half a bay leaf, celery stalk, salt, thyme, and water. Bring to a boil, reduce heat, cover, and simmer until chicken is very tender (1¼ to 1½ hours). Strain and reserve broth; measure 1½ cups of the broth for pie and freeze remainder for another use. Remove chicken from bones, discarding bones, skin, and vegetables. Divide chicken into generous bite-sized pieces (about 3 cups).

Cornmeal Pastry In a large bowl mix flour, cornmeal, and salt. Cut in butter and lard until mixture forms coarse crumbs. Beat egg yolk with water (reserve egg white to glaze pastry); gradually mix into flour mixture, stirring with a fork until pastry clings together. Shape with your hands into a smooth ball. Roll out on a floured board or pastry cloth to a circle about 12 inches in diameter.

HAM AND CHEESE CUSTARD PIE

Quichelike, this creamy breakast pie is baked in a crisp rye pastry.

- 2 tablespoons butter
- ½ pound thinly sliced baked or boiled ham, cut in thin strips
- ¼ cup grated Parmesan cheese
- 5 eggs
- 1 cup sour cream
- ½ teaspoon salt
  Pinch each ground nutmeg and white pepper

Rye Pastry

- 1 cup all-purpose flour
- ¼ cup rye flour
- ¼ teaspoon salt
- ¼ cup cold butter or margarine
- 2 tablespoons lard or soft shortening
- 1 egg yolk
- 2 tablespoons cold water

1. Preheat oven to 450° F. Melt butter in a large frying pan over medium heat and cook ham, stirring occasionally, until lightly browned. Spoon evenly into Rye Pastry shell. Sprinkle with cheese.

2. Beat eggs well with sour cream, salt, nutmeg, and white pepper. Pour over ham and cheese.

3. Bake for 10 minutes; reduce heat to 350° F and continue baking until crust is nicely browned and filling is just set in center (20 to 25 minutes). Let stand about 3 minutes before cutting in wedges to serve.

Serves 6.

Rye Pastry In a large bowl mix flours and salt. Cut in butter and lard until mixture forms coarse crumbs. Beat egg yolk with water; gradually mix into flour mixture, stirring with a fork until pastry clings together. Shape with your hands into a smooth ball. Roll out on a floured board or pastry cloth to a circle. Fit pastry into a 9-inch pie pan; trim and flute edge.

BLUE CHEESE QUICHE

Any blue-veined cheese will give this creamy quiche a wonderfully piquant flavor, but try true French Roquefort.

- ½ cup crumbled blue-veined cheese
- 1 cup grated Swiss cheese
  Egg Pastry for Quiche, unbaked (see page 100)
- 2 tablespoons butter
- 2 shallots, finely chopped or ¼ cup finely chopped mild onion
- 4 eggs
- 1 cup half-and-half
- 1 teaspoon Dijon mustard
- ½ teaspoon salt
- ¼ teaspoon each paprika and ground nutmeg
  Pinch white pepper

1. Preheat oven to 450° F. Distribute cheeses evenly in Egg Pastry shell. In a small frying pan over medium heat melt butter and cook shallots until soft and golden; sprinkle mixture over cheese.

2. Beat eggs with half-and-half, mustard, salt, paprika, nutmeg, and white pepper; pour over cheese.

3. Bake quiche for 10 minutes; reduce heat to 350° F and continue baking until quiche is nicely browned and just set in center (20 to 25 minutes longer).

4. Let stand about 3 minutes before cutting in wedges to serve.

Serves 6.

FRESH SALMON QUICHE

Fresh salmon, lightly steamed, makes this splendid quiche a good choice for a spring or summer brunch. You might accompany it with a green salad containing sliced papaya and mixed with a lime juice and oil dressing.

- ½ pound salmon fillet
- 2 tablespoons butter
- 4 green onions, thinly sliced
- ½ teaspoon dried dillweed
  Egg Pastry for Quiche, unbaked (see page 100)
- 1 cup grated Swiss cheese
- 3 eggs
- 1 cup half-and-half
- ¾ teaspoon salt
- ½ teaspoon dry mustard
  Pinch white pepper

1. Preheat oven to 450° F. Place salmon on a rack over about ½ inch of water in a medium frying pan. Bring water to a boil, cover, reduce heat, and steam until salmon flakes when tested with a fork (6 to 8 minutes). Remove and discard skin and flake salmon gently.

2. In a medium frying pan over moderate heat melt butter and cook green onions until limp and bright green (about 3 minutes). Remove from heat; mix in salmon and dillweed. Distribute salmon mixture evenly in Egg Pastry shell. Sprinkle with cheese.

3. Beat eggs with half-and-half, salt, dry mustard, and white pepper; pour over cheese.

4. Bake quiche for 10 minutes; reduce heat to 350° F and continue baking until crust is nicely browned and filling is just set in center (20 to 25 minutes longer).

5. Let stand about 3 minutes before cutting in wedges to serve.

Serves 6.

SAVORY FILO-WRAPPED PASTRIES

For these filo dough–wrapped pastries, use the paper-thin sheets of filo sold in 1-pound packages, refrigerated or frozen, in your supermarket or in stores that feature Greek and other ethnic foods. A package of filo is a versatile ingredient to keep in the freezer, since it can be used for a number of breakfast pastries.

GREEK SPINACH PIE

Buttery-crisp layers of filo dough make an irresistible vegetable pie known in Greece as *spanokopita*. For a fully Greek-inspired brunch add tiny lamb chops grilled with olive oil and oregano, with lemon to squeeze over; a loaf of sesame-seeded bread; and a salad of tomatoes, cucumber, pepper strips, and ripe olives.

> 2 *bunches (about ¾ lb each) spinach*
> ¼ *cup olive oil*
> 1 *medium onion, finely chopped*
> 1 *bunch (6 to 8) green onions, thinly sliced (use part of tops)*
> 1 *tablespoon dried dillweed*
> ½ *cup finely chopped parsley*
> 4 *eggs*
> ¾ *teaspoon salt*
> ⅛ *teaspoon each freshly ground pepper and ground nutmeg*
> 1¾ *cups crumbled feta cheese (½ lb)*
> ½ *pound filo dough, thawed if frozen*
> ¾ *cup butter, melted*

1. Remove and discard stems from spinach and wash; you should have about 4 quarts leaves. Set aside.

2. In a large frying pan over medium heat, heat olive oil and cook onion and green onions until soft and golden. Remove with a slotted spoon and reserve. To oil in same pan add spinach, lifting and turning for 1 to 3 minutes, just until leaves are wilted. Drain spinach well, pressing out moisture; chop coarsely. Add to onion mixture with dillweed and parsley.

3. In a large bowl beat eggs with salt, pepper, and nutmeg. Lightly mix in vegetable mixture and cheese.

4. Unfold sheets of filo dough so they lie flat. Cover with plastic wrap, then a damp towel, to prevent them from drying out. Brush a 9- by 13-inch pan generously with some of the melted butter. Line pan with 1 sheet of filo, brush with melted butter, and cover with 5 more sheets of filo, brushing each with melted butter and letting filo overlap sides of pan.

5. Pour in spinach mixture, spreading it evenly. Fold overhanging filo back over spinach. Top with remaining sheets of filo dough, each folded to fit pan and brushed with butter. Brush top with any remaining butter. Using a razor blade or small, sharp knife, cut through top layers of filo to mark 24 squares. (If made ahead, cover and refrigerate.)

6. Preheat oven to 350° F. Bake, uncovered, until pastry is well browned (45 minutes to 1 hour). Place pan on a rack to cool slightly, then finish cutting into squares, following the original cuts. Serve warm or at room temperature.

Makes 24 pieces.

CHICKEN AND VEAL FILO ROLLS

These walnut-accented nuggets are delicious for brunch with white wine, buttered carrots, and sweet pickles.

> 2 *whole chicken breasts (4 halves, about 2 lbs total), boned and skinned*
> 2 *tablespoons butter or margarine*
> 1 *small onion, finely chopped*
> 2 *tablespoons brandy*
> 1 *egg*
> ¼ *cup soft bread crumbs*
> 1 *teaspoon salt*
> ⅛ *teaspoon each white pepper and ground allspice*
> 1 *pound ground veal or turkey*
> ¼ *cup chopped parsley*
> ⅓ *cup coarsely chopped toasted walnuts*
> 12 *sheets (about ½ lb) filo dough, thawed if frozen*
> ½ *cup butter or margarine, melted*

1. Cut chicken breasts crosswise into ½-inch strips. In a large frying pan over medium heat, melt the 2 tablespoons butter and cook chicken strips and onion, stirring often, until lightly browned. Mix in brandy and cook, stirring, until most of the liquid is gone. Remove from heat.

2. In a large bowl beat egg slightly; mix in bread crumbs, salt, white pepper, and allspice. Then lightly mix in veal, parsley, walnuts, and chicken mixture.

3. Unfold sheets of filo dough so they lie flat. Cover with plastic wrap, then a damp towel, to prevent them from drying out. Remove one sheet of filo at a time, brush half with the melted butter, and fold in half to make a rectangle about 9 by 12 inches. Brush again with butter.

4. Shape about ⅓ cup of the chicken mixture into a roll and place at narrow end of dough. Fold in sides of filo about 1½ inches and roll up. Place seam side down on greased or nonstick baking sheets. Repeat for remaining dough and filling. (If made ahead, cover and refrigerate.) Brush with remaining butter.

5. Preheat oven to 350° F. Bake until golden brown (30 to 35 minutes). Serve hot.

Makes 12 rolls.

BAKED BREAKFAST REUBENS

These rectangular pastries enclose corned beef, sauerkraut, and Swiss cheese in a flaky filo wrapping.

12 *sheets (about ½ lb) filo dough, thawed if frozen*
6 *tablespoons to ½ cup butter or margarine, melted*
12 *thin slices corned beef*
1 *can (8 oz) sauerkraut, drained*
½ *pound thinly sliced Swiss cheese*

Russian Dressing

¼ *cup mayonnaise*
1 *tablespoon chili sauce*
 Pinch cayenne pepper
2 *tablespoons finely chopped stuffed olives*

1. Unfold sheets of filo dough so they lie flat. Cover with plastic wrap, then a damp towel, to prevent them from drying out. Remove one sheet of filo at a time, brush half lightly with melted butter, and fold in half to make a rectangle about 9 by 12 inches. Brush again with butter.

2. At one narrow end place slice of corned beef, folded to make about a 3- by 5-inch rectangle. Top with a dollop of Russian Dressing, sauerkraut, and cheese (folded to same size as corned beef). Fold in sides of filo about 1½ inches then, starting at end with filling, turn over 3 times to make an envelope-shaped packet. Place seam side down on greased baking sheet. (If made ahead, cover and refrigerate.) Brush with butter.

3. Preheat oven to 350° F. Bake until golden brown (20 to 25 minutes). Serve hot.

Makes 12 sandwiches.

Russian Dressing Mix all ingredients.

Makes a scant ½ cup.

FILLED LOAVES AND PASTRIES

Enclosing foods in a crust, or *en croûte*, makes a handsome presentation. A buttery brioche dough is simple to stir up and use as a wrapping.

RATATOUILLE IN A WHOLE WHEAT SHELL

Complement the robust red pepper and eggplant filling with grilled garlic sausages and a green salad.

¼ *cup olive oil*
1 *small unpeeled eggplant (about 1 lb), cut in ½-inch cubes*
1 *medium onion, slivered*
½ *pound mushrooms, thinly sliced*
1 *sweet red or green bell pepper, seeded and cut in strips*
1 *clove garlic, minced or pressed*
¾ *teaspoon each dried basil and dried oregano*
½ *teaspoon salt*
⅛ *teaspoon pepper*
 Pinch cayenne pepper
1 *can (1 lb) tomatoes*
2 *eggs*
¼ *cup grated Parmesan cheese*
1 *cup grated Swiss cheese*
1 *egg, beaten with 1 teaspoon water*

Wheat Dough

1 *package active dry yeast*
¼ *cup warm water*
1 *tablespoon honey*
½ *teaspoon salt*
1½ *cups all-purpose flour*
2 *eggs*
½ *cup whole wheat flour*
½ *cup butter, softened*

1. Prepare Wheat Dough and, while it is rising, make filling.

2. In a large frying pan over medium heat, heat olive oil and cook eggplant and onion, stirring often, until vegetables are soft (about 10 minutes). Add mushrooms and red pepper; cook, stirring occasionally, until

mushrooms brown lightly. Mix in garlic, basil, oregano, salt, pepper, cayenne, and tomatoes (coarsely chopped) and their liquid.

3. Bring mixture to a boil, reduce heat, and simmer, stirring occasionally, until mixture is thick and reduced to about 4 cups (20 to 25 minutes). Remove from heat and let cool for about 10 minutes.

4. Beat the 2 eggs slightly in a medium bowl. Mix lightly into vegetable mixture with cheeses.

5. With well-floured hands shape about two thirds of the dough into a ball. Roll out on a generously floured board or pastry cloth to about a 14-inch circle. Line a well-greased 8-inch springform pan with dough.

6. Spread vegetable mixture in dough-lined pan. Fold edge of dough down over edge of filling. Roll out remaining dough to a circle a little larger than the pan. Place over filling; moisten edges and press together with a fork to seal.

7. Cover lightly with waxed paper and let rise in a warm place until dough looks puffy (30 to 45 minutes).

8. Preheat oven to 375° F. Brush lightly with egg mixture. Bake until dough is richly browned and sounds hollow when tapped (about 1 hour).

9. Let stand in pan on a rack for about 15 minutes before removing sides of pan. Cut in wedges and serve warm or at room temperature.

Serves 8.

Wheat Dough Sprinkle yeast over water in large bowl of electric mixer; let stand for 5 minutes to soften. Mix in honey and salt, then ½ cup of the all-purpose flour. Beat at medium speed until elastic (about 3 minutes). Beat in eggs, one at a time, until smooth, then gradually beat in whole wheat flour and remaining 1 cup all-purpose flour. Add butter, 1 tablespoon at a a time, beating well after each addition. Transfer to a greased bowl, cover, and let rise until doubled (about 1½ hours). Stir dough down.

PATIO BRUNCH

Mimosas (see page 23)

Sweet Corn and Bacon Quiche

Sliced Tomatoes

Fresh Strawberry Torte

Coffee

Summertime produce—sweet corn, juicy strawberries—are featured in the two special dishes of this warm-weather brunch. As guests arrive and the quiche finishes baking, offer them Mimosas, lovely froths of Champagne and fresh orange juice to sip.

To keep last-minute preparations to a minimum, have the unbaked Cornmeal Pastry Shell containing corn, cheese, and bacon ready.

SWEET CORN AND BACON QUICHE

6 slices bacon, cut crosswise in ½-inch strips
2 ears corn, kernels cut from cobs (1½ to 2 cups corn)
1 cup grated Cheddar cheese
5 eggs
1½ cups half-and-half
½ teaspoon salt
Pinch cayenne pepper

Cornmeal Pastry Shell

1 cup flour
¼ cup yellow cornmeal
¼ teaspoon salt
2 tablespoons grated Parmesan cheese
¼ cup butter or margarine
2 tablespoons lard
1 egg

1. Preheat oven to 450° F. Cook bacon until lightly browned; drain on paper towel.

2. In Cornmeal Pastry Shell, evenly distribute corn, cheese, and bacon. Beat eggs with half-and-half, salt, and cayenne. Pour egg mixture over corn, cheese, and bacon.

3. Bake quiche for 10 minutes; reduce heat to 350° F and continue baking until quiche is nicely browned and just set in center (20 to 25 minutes longer).

4. Let stand for about 3 minutes before cutting in wedges to serve.

Serves 6 to 8.

Cornmeal Pastry Shell In a medium bowl mix flour, cornmeal, salt, and cheese. Cut in butter and lard until mixture is crumbly. Beat egg; gradually add to flour mixture, stirring until it is evenly moistened and begins to cling together. Shape into a flattened ball. Roll out on a floured board or pastry cloth to about a 13-inch circle. Fit pastry into a 10-inch quiche dish, trimming about ½ inch above top edge. Then press edge under, even with top of dish.

FRESH STRAWBERRY TORTE

Almond Press-In Pastry (see page 109)
4 cups strawberries
1 cup granulated sugar
2 tablespoons each cornstarch and lemon juice
1 cup whipping cream
2 teaspooons confectioners' sugar
Dash vanilla extract
2 tablespoons toasted sliced almonds

1. Preheat oven to 425° F. Press Almond Press-In Pastry into the bottom and halfway up the sides of a 9-inch springform pan. Using a fork, pierce sides and bottom of the pastry. Bake until lightly browned (10 to 12 minutes). Cool in pan on a wire rack.

2. Remove and discard hulls from strawberries, reserving three with leaves for garnish. Place half of the strawberries in a medium saucepan and crush them with a fork. Mix in granulated sugar, cornstarch, and lemon juice. Cook over medium heat, stirring, until thickened and transparent (about 10 minutes). Cool until lukewarm.

3. Cut remaining strawberries into halves; fold them into cooked strawberry mixture. Spread filling in pastry shell and refrigerate until filling is set (1 to 2 hours). Cover if refrigerated any longer.

4. Remove sides of pan. Whip cream with confectioners' sugar and vanilla until stiff. Spread or mound over strawberry filling. Sprinkle with almonds. Garnish with leaved berries. Cut in wedges to serve.

Serves 8 to 10.

Pie lovers take notice—this menu for a warm-weather brunch presents two of them: Sweet Corn and Bacon Quiche and Fresh Strawberry Torte.

PROVENÇAL TOMATO GALETTES

The French eat a *galette* (a sweet or savory filled turnover) as a snack or lunch, but you will find these delightful for brunch. Made with packaged puff pastry, they go together quickly. Accompany them with Elegant Oranges (see page 30) for a first course; then serve crisp raw vegetables—radishes and carrot and cucumber sticks—on ice with the turnovers.

    ¼ cup olive oil
     2 large onions, slivered
     1 large can (28 oz) tomatoes
     ½ teaspoon each sugar, salt,
        and dried rosemary
    ⅛ teaspoon cayenne pepper
     1 clove garlic, minced or pressed
     1 cup julienned ham
     1 package (17¼ oz) frozen puff
        pastry, thawed for 20 minutes
    24 tiny Niçoise olives or halved,
        pitted ripe olives
     1 egg, beaten with 1 teaspoon
        water

1. Preheat oven to 400° F. In a large frying pan over medium heat, heat 2 tablespoons of the olive oil and cook onions, stirring occasionally, until soft and lightly browned. Remove with a slotted spoon and reserve.

2. Heat remaining 2 tablespoons olive oil in same pan. Add tomatoes (coarsely chopped) and their liquid, sugar, salt, rosemary, cayenne, and garlic. Cook over high heat, stirring occasionally, until mixture is thickened and reduced to about 2 cups. Mix in ham.

3. Roll each sheet of puff pastry out on a floured board or pastry cloth to a 12-inch square. Divide each piece of pastry into four 6-inch squares. On each square place an eighth of the onions and about ¼ cup of the tomato sauce. Top each with 3 olives.

Bring opposite corners of each square to meet in center, pinching together in center and at edges to hold. Place on greased or nonstick baking sheets. Brush lightly with egg mixture.

4. Bake until pastry is well browned (15 to 18 minutes).

Serves 8.

HOT PORK AND HAM PÂTÉ IN BRIOCHE

French through and through, this hot pâté is baked inside a buttery brioche dough. The tart little pickles called *cornichons* complement its garlic-accented flavor, as do creamed spinach and a sprightly young red wine such as a French Beaujolais.

     2 tablespoons butter
     1 large onion, finely chopped
     1 clove garlic, minced or pressed
    ¼ cup brandy
     1 egg
     ½ cup soft bread crumbs
     1 pound ground pork
     2 cups ground baked ham
    ¼ cup finely chopped parsley
     ½ teaspoon each salt and
        dried thyme
    ¼ teaspoon ground allspice
    ⅛ teaspoon white pepper
     1 egg, beaten with 1 teaspoon
        water

Brioche Dough

     1 package dry yeast
    ¼ cup warm water
     1 tablespoon sugar
     ½ teaspoon salt
     2 cups flour
     2 eggs
     ½ cup butter or margarine,
        softened

1. Prepare Brioche Dough and, while it is rising, make filling.

2. In a medium frying pan, melt butter and cook onion until soft but not browned. Mix in garlic and brandy; cook, stirring, until most of the liquid cooks away.

3. Beat the 1 egg in a large bowl. Mix in bread crumbs, then ground meats, onion mixture, parsley, salt, thyme, allspice, and white pepper. Cover and refrigerate until ready to enclose in dough.

4. Roll dough out on a generously floured board or pastry cloth to make a rectangle about 10 by 20 inches. Shape filling with your hands into a loaf about 4 by 8 inches. Place filling at one end of dough. Pinch dough to seal ends. Place, with long sealed edge at bottom, in a well-greased 5- by 9-inch loaf pan.

5. Cover lightly with waxed paper and let rise in a warm place until dough looks puffy (about 30 minutes). Or, cover and refrigerate for several hours or overnight; remove from refrigerator about 1 hour (until puffy looking) before baking.

6. Preheat oven to 350° F. Brush lightly with beaten egg mixture. Bake until dough is well browned and juice runs clear when a long skewer is inserted in center (about 1½ hours).

7. Place pâté (still in pan) on a rack and let stand for about 15 minutes; then carefully remove loaf from pan and cut into 1-inch-thick slices. Serve warm.

Serves 6 to 8.

Brioche Dough Sprinkle yeast over water in large bowl of electric mixer; let stand for 5 minutes to soften. Mix in sugar and salt, then ½ cup of the flour. Beat at medium speed until elastic (about 3 minutes). Beat in eggs, one at a time, until smooth, then gradually beat in remaining 1½ cups flour. Add butter, 1 tablespoon at a time, beating well after each addition. Transfer to a greased bowl, cover, and let rise in a warm place until doubled (about 1½ hours). Stir dough down.

FRUIT TARTS

People who aren't expert pastry chefs sometimes avoid attempting sweet pies. But if you use a tender press-in pastry (plain or with ground nuts for part of its substance) for fruit pies, you will be pleasantly surprised by the quality of crust you can achieve.

RHUBARB MERINGUE TART

Baked in a large, round tart pan, this fresh rhubarb pie makes a handsome presentation for a spring brunch.

    3 eggs, separated
    1 cup sugar
    2 tablespoons flour
    ⅛ teaspoon ground nutmeg
    ½ teaspoon grated orange rind
    ¼ cup each orange juice and
       whipping cream
    4 cups diced rhubarb

Press-In Pastry

    1½ cups flour
    ¼ cup sugar
    ½ cup cold butter or margarine
    1 egg yolk
    ½ teaspoon vanilla extract

Meringue

    3 egg whites (reserved from
       yolks used in filling)
    ⅛ teaspoon cream of tartar
    ¼ cup sugar

1. Preheat oven to 450° F. Press pastry into bottom and up the sides of an 11-inch removable-bottom, round tart pan.

2. Separate eggs and set aside whites to use in meringue. Beat egg yolks and sugar until thick and pale; blend in flour, nutmeg, and orange rind, then orange juice and cream. Fold in rhubarb, mixing lightly to coat. Spread in Press-In Pastry shell.

3. Bake for 10 minutes; reduce heat to 350° F and bake until filling is set and rhubarb is tender (25 to 30 minutes). Remove tart from oven.

4. Spread Meringue lightly over rhubarb filling. Return to 350° F oven and bake until meringue is a pale golden brown (8 to 10 minutes).

5. Remove pan sides and serve tart warm or at room temperature.

Serves 6 to 8.

Press-In Pastry Mix flour with sugar. Cut in butter until crumbly. Beat egg yolk with vanilla. With a fork, stir egg mixture lightly into flour mixture. Using hands, press dough into smooth, flat ball.

Meringue Beat egg whites until frothy; beat in cream of tartar and continue beating until soft peaks form. Gradually add sugar, beating until mixture is stiff and glossy.

FRESH PLUM KUCHEN

Early autumn's fresh, small, blue prune plums bake to crimson juiciness in this sugar-sprinkled dessert.

       Press-In Pastry (see above)
    ⅔ cup sugar
    ¼ teaspoon ground nutmeg
    3 tablespoons flour
    1 tablespoon lemon juice
    4 cups small blue prune plums,
       halved and pitted
    1 tablespoon butter or
       margarine
       Sugar
       Crème fraîche or sour cream

1. Preheat oven to 375° F. Press pastry into the bottom and about halfway up the sides of a 9-inch springform pan.

2. Mix sugar, nutmeg, and flour. Stir lemon juice into plums in a bowl, then mix lightly with sugar mixture. Arrange fruit, cut sides up, making 2 layers in pastry-lined pan. Sprinkle with any sugar mixture remaining in bowl. Dot with butter.

3. Bake on lowest rack of oven until pastry is well browned and plums are tender and bubbling (50 minutes to 1 hour). Sprinkle with sugar.

4. Remove pan sides and serve tart warm or cool with crème fraîche or sour cream spooned over each piece.

Serves 6 to 8.

FRESH APRICOT TART

Delight brunch guests with this almond-sprinkled fruit tart.

    4 cups halved, pitted apricots
       (about 2 lbs)
    ⅓ cup sugar
    1 teaspoon cornstarch
    ⅛ teaspoon ground nutmeg
    2 tablespoons butter or
       margarine
    ⅔ cup apricot preserves
    1 tablespoon orange-flavored
       liqueur
    ¼ cup toasted sliced almonds

Almond Press-In Pastry

    1¼ cups flour
    ¼ cup each ground blanched
       almonds (whirled in blender
       or food processor until
       powdery) and sugar
    ½ cup cold butter or margarine
    1 egg yolk
    ¼ teaspoon each vanilla extract
       and almond extract

1. Preheat oven to 450° F. Press Almond Press-In Pastry into bottom and up the sides of an 11-inch removable-bottom, round tart pan.

2. Arrange apricots, cut sides down and overlapping slightly, in pastry-lined pan. Mix sugar, cornstarch, and nutmeg; sprinkle over apricots. Dot with butter.

3. Bake for 12 minutes; reduce heat to 350° F and bake until apricots are tender and crust is brown (25 to 30 minutes). Cool in pan on a wire rack.

4. Heat preserves until melted and bubbling; strain out solid pieces of fruit. Mix in liqueur. Spoon glaze over apricots. Sprinkle edge with almonds to make a 2-inch border.

5. Remove pan sides to serve tart at room temperature.

Serves 6 to 8.

Almond Press-In Pastry Mix flour with almonds and sugar. Cut in butter until crumbly. Blend egg yolk with vanilla and almond extract. With a fork, stir egg mixture lightly into flour mixture. Using hands, press dough into smooth, flat ball.

*Yeast breads, clockwise from left:
Honey-Wheat Toasting Bread,
Braided Egg Bread, Italian
Sausage Bread, and Filbert
Loaves. Recipes begin on 118.*

Breads & Cakes

Bread is the mainstay of many breakfasts. When you bake it in your own kitchen, you can count on fragrant bread to coax slugabeds to the breakfast table. Bake breads at your convenience, freeze them while they are at their peak, then thaw and reheat them later to dazzle family and friends at breakfast or brunch. This chapter includes both quick breads—muffins, scones, popovers, fruit-and-nut breads, and easy coffee cakes—and yeast breads: hearty whole grain loaves, an elegant braided egg bread, beaten-batter breads, croissants, and some tempting sweet rolls.

Cakelike Miniature Cinnamon Muffins are tiny two-bite-sized temptations. Serve them warm, with fruity Orange Spiced Tea (page 18), for brunch or an afternoon break.

QUICK BREADS

The designation *quick bread* includes muffins, fruit and nut breads, and easy coffee cakes. What they have in common is a leavening of baking powder or baking soda. That means that these breads can be stirred together in a few minutes and baked at once, without the lengthy rising period yeast breads need.

MINIATURE CINNAMON MUFFINS

These delicate currant-studded muffins are dipped while warm from the oven in butter and cinnamon-sugar. Snugly wrapped to stay warm, they are an irresistible feature of a brunch buffet.

1½ cups flour
1½ teaspoons baking powder
¼ teaspoon each *salt and ground nutmeg*
¼ cup dried currants
⅓ cup butter or margarine, softened
½ cup sugar
½ teaspoon vanilla extract
1 egg
½ cup milk
6 tablespoons butter or margarine, melted

Cinnamon-Sugar

½ cup sugar
1 teaspoon ground cinnamon

1. Preheat oven to 375° F. In a medium bowl mix flour, baking powder, salt, nutmeg, and dried currants.

2. In large bowl electric mixer cream the ⅓ cup butter with sugar, then beat in vanilla and egg until well combined. Add flour mixture to butter mixture alternately with milk, mixing after each addition just until combined.

3. Fill greased 1¾-inch muffin pans two-thirds full.

4. Bake until muffins are golden brown (18 to 20 minutes). Remove hot muffins from pans at once and dip quickly into the melted butter, then roll in Cinnamon-Sugar to coat. Serve warm.

Makes 2 dozen 1¾-inch muffins.

Cinnamon-Sugar In a small bowl thoroughly combine sugar and cinnamon.

ORANGE MARMALADE MUFFINS

Muffins are one of the fastest quick breads and with only a little planning, you can stir up a batch even on a weekday morning. Have muffin pans greased and ready to use. Then quickly combine the liquid and dry mixtures, and spoon the batter into the pans. In less than half an hour the muffins will be ready to eat, temptingly hot.

This recipe also includes three variations: savory Cheddar Cheese Muffins with sesame seeds, moist Apple-Pecan Muffins, and tart, fresh Spiced Cranberry Muffins.

> 2 cups flour
> ¼ cup sugar
> 1 tablespoon baking powder
> ½ teaspoon salt
> 1 egg
> 1 cup milk
> 3 tablespoons butter or margarine, melted, or salad oil
> 2 teaspoons grated orange rind
> ⅓ cup orange marmalade

1. Preheat oven to 400° F. In a large bowl stir together flour, sugar, baking powder, and salt.

2. In a medium bowl beat egg with milk, melted butter, and orange rind. Add egg mixture to flour mixture, stirring only until flour is moistened.

3. Fill greased 2½-inch muffin pans one-third full. To each, add about 1 teaspoon of marmalade. Use remaining batter to fill pans two-thirds full.

4. Bake until well browned (20 to 25 minutes). Serve warm.

Makes 1 dozen muffins.

Cheddar Cheese Muffins Omit orange rind and marmalade. Decrease sugar to 2 tablespoons. To flour mixture add 1 cup grated Cheddar cheese. After filling greased muffin pans two-thirds full with cheese batter, sprinkle muffins lightly with sesame seeds.

Apple-Pecan Muffins Omit orange rind and marmalade. Increase sugar to ⅓ cup. To flour mixture add ½ teaspoon ground cinnamon and ¼ cup finely chopped pecans. To egg mixture add 1 small tart apple (peeled, cored, and shredded). Sprinkle each muffin lightly with about 1 teaspoon pecans before baking. Bake for a total of 25 to 30 minutes.

Spiced Cranberry Muffins Omit marmalade. Coarsely chop ¾ cup fresh cranberries; measure ½ cup sugar, and mix ⅓ cup of it into cranberries in a small bowl. Let stand while preparing muffin batter. In flour mixture use the remaining measured sugar (2 tablespoons plus 2 teaspoons) in place of the ¼ cup called for in basic recipe. To flour mixture add ½ teaspoon ground cinnamon and ¼ teaspoon ground nutmeg. After adding the egg mixture to the flour mixture, stir in cranberry mixture with last few strokes. Increase baking time to a total of 25 to 30 minutes.

Welcome the morning with a basket of warm Apple-Pecan Muffins. Serving these goodies needn't deprive the cook of beauty sleep. Like most of the breads in this chapter, they can be made ahead, frozen, and then reheated when needed.

ORANGE-DATE MUFFINS

Moist and dense with chopped fresh orange, walnuts, and dates, these muffins have a deliciously fresh flavor. Serve them with a fruit salad and Hot Chocolate (page 18) for a well-rounded breakfast.

    1 small orange
    1 cup flour
    ¼ teaspoon each *salt and
       baking powder*
    ½ teaspoon baking soda
    ·¾ teaspoon ground cinnamon
    ½ cup finely chopped walnuts
    ⅓ cup chopped dates
    1 egg
    ½ cup firmly packed
       brown sugar
    ⅓ cup salad oil
    ½ teaspoon vanilla extract

1. Preheat oven to 375° F. Grate and reserve rind from orange. Then cut off and discard any remaining rind and all white membrane from orange. Finely chop orange (discard seeds if any) and add grated rind. Measure and add orange juice, if necessary, to make ⅔ cup.

2. In a large bowl mix flour, salt, baking powder, soda, cinnamon, walnuts, and dates. In a medium bowl beat egg with brown sugar and oil until blended. Mix in vanilla and orange mixture.

3. Add egg mixture to flour mixture, stirring only until flour is moistened. Fill greased 2½-inch muffin pans two-thirds full.

4. Bake until muffins are well browned and a wooden toothpick inserted in centers comes out clean (20 to 25 minutes). Serve warm or at room temperature.

Makes 1 dozen muffins.

MAPLE-NUT BRAN MUFFINS

These layered bran muffins include a luxurious touch—real maple sugar in the cinnamon-walnut filling. If it is not available, you can substitute brown sugar.

    1   cup whole-bran cereal
    ¾   cup milk
    1   egg
    ¼   cup soft shortening
    1   cup flour
    2½ teaspoons baking powder
    ½   teaspoon salt
    ¼   cup sugar

Maple-Nut Filling

    ½ cup packed maple sugar
       or brown sugar
    ½ cup finely chopped walnuts
    2 tablespoons flour
    ½ teaspoon ground cinnamon

1. Preheat oven to 400° F. In a medium bowl combine cereal and milk; let stand until most of the liquid is absorbed. Beat in egg and shortening.

2. In a large bowl mix flour, baking powder, salt, and sugar. Add cereal mixture, mixing only until combined.

3. Spoon a small amount of batter into 12 compartments in greased or nonstick 2½-inch muffin pans; sprinkle with some of the filling. Repeat layers until pans are about three-fourths full.

4. Bake until muffins are well browned (20 to 25 minutes). Serve warm.

Makes 1 dozen muffins.

Maple-Nut Filling Mix maple sugar, walnuts, flour, and cinnamon.

AUNTIE'S SCONES

A scone (it rhymes with gone) is a sweet, buttery biscuit with a British background. Buttermilk makes these remarkably crisp crusted, yet moist within.

    2   cups flour
    1   teaspoon cream of tartar
    ½   teaspoon baking soda
    ⅛   teaspoon salt
    ¼   cup sugar
    ½   cup cold butter or margarine
    ¼ to ⅓ cup buttermilk

Warm Honey Butter

    1 cup each *butter and honey*

1. Preheat oven to 350° F. In a medium bowl stir together flour, cream of tartar, baking soda, salt, and sugar. Cut in butter until mixture has a uniform consistency of coarse crumbs.

2. Gradually stir in buttermilk, 1 tablespoon at a time, just until mixture is moist enough to cling together. (Too much mixing or too much liquid will make the scones tough.)

3. With floured hands, lightly shape dough into a flattened ball. Roll out on a floured board or pastry cloth to a circle about 8 inches in diameter and ½ inch thick. Using a floured 2½-inch cutter, cut into rounds. Place on a greased or nonstick baking sheet.

4. Bake until golden brown (15 to 20 minutes).

5. Serve warm, split and drizzled with warm Honey Butter.

Makes 10 to 12 scones.

Honey Butter In a small pan over medium heat, combine butter and honey, stirring until blended and hot.

Makes about ½ cup.

CRISP POPOVERS

A popover is a stunning quick bread—billowing and crusty. A successfully executed popover is nearly all outside, with a perfectly hollow interior. That means it has lots of space to fill with butter and jam, or something as substantial as creamed poultry or seafood.

This recipe has a handy feature. The batter can be made ahead in your blender or food processor, then refrigerated for hours or overnight before baking. Avoid opening the oven until popovers are nearly at the end of their baking time.

> 1 cup milk
> 2 eggs
> 1 tablespoon butter, melted, or salad oil
> 1 cup flour
> ¼ teaspoon salt
> 1 tablespoon sugar

1. Generously butter 2½-inch muffin or popover pans.

2. In blender or food processor, combine milk, eggs, butter, flour, salt, and sugar. Whirl until smooth and well combined, stopping motor and scraping flour from sides of container once or twice. (If made ahead, cover and refrigerate. Stir batter well before using.) Preheat oven to 400° F. Pour batter into prepared pans, filling them about half full.

3. Bake (avoid opening oven during baking) until popovers are well browned and firm to the touch (35 to 40 minutes). Serve hot.

Makes 10 to 12 popovers.

LEMON DROP TEACAKE

Lots of fresh lemon flavors this pretty, syrup-soaked ground almond cake. Inside, it is moist with yogurt.

> 1 cup butter, softened
> 1 cup sugar
> 1½ teaspoons grated lemon rind
> 1 teaspoon vanilla extract
> 4 eggs (at room temperature)
> 2½ cups flour
> 1 teaspoon each baking powder and baking soda
> ¼ teaspoon salt
> 1 cup finely ground blanched almonds (whirled in blender or food processor until powdery)
> 1 cup plain yogurt

Lemon Syrup

> ½ cup sugar
> ⅓ cup lemon juice
> 2 tablespoons water

1. Preheat oven to 350° F. In a large bowl cream butter and sugar until fluffy. Beat in lemon rind and vanilla, then add eggs, one at a time, beating well after each addition.

2. Mix flour, baking powder, soda, salt, and almonds. Add flour mixture to butter mixture alternately with yogurt, beating well after each addition.

3. Pour batter into a well-greased, lightly floured 8½- to 9-inch bundt pan or other 9-cup tube pan.

4. Bake until cake pulls away from sides of pan and tests done when a long skewer is inserted in thickest part (50 to 60 minutes). Using a fork, pierce surface of cake all over. Slowly pour Lemon Syrup over hot cake. Let cake cool in pan on a wire rack.

5. Invert cake onto a plate to cut and serve.

Serves 8 to 10.

Lemon Syrup In a small saucepan combine sugar, lemon juice, and water and stir over medium heat until sugar dissolves and mixture boils. Boil for 2 minutes. Keep warm until ready to use.

BANANA-NUT COFFEE CAKE

A crumbly brown sugar and walnut mixture tops this spicy, orange-accented banana cake.

> ¼ cup butter or margarine, softened
> ⅓ cup sugar
> 1 soft ripe banana, mashed (about ½ cup)
> ¼ cup sour cream
> 1 egg
> 2 teaspoons grated orange rind
> 1¼ cups flour
> 1 tablespoon baking soda
> ¼ teaspoon each salt and ground nutmeg
> ¼ cup milk
> ⅓ cup chopped walnuts

Brown Sugar Streusel

> ¼ cup each flour and firmly packed brown sugar
> 2 tablespoons granulated sugar
> ½ teaspoon ground cinnamon
> 3 tablespoons cold butter or margarine

1. Preheat oven to 375° F. In large bowl of electric mixer, cream butter and sugar until fluffy; blend in banana, sour cream, egg, and orange rind.

2. Mix flour, baking powder, soda, salt, and nutmeg. Stir flour mixture into banana mixture alternately with milk, blending after each addition just until combined. Spread in a greased 8-inch square baking pan.

3. Sprinkle evenly with Brown Sugar Streusel, then with walnuts.

4. Bake until wooden toothpick inserted in center comes out clean (35 to 40 minutes). Let cool slightly before cutting into squares. Serve warm or at room temperature.

Makes 1 coffee cake.

Brown Sugar Streusel In a small bowl mix flour, sugars, and cinnamon. Cut in butter until coarse crumbs form.

A layer of spiced walnuts swirls through the center of this sugar-dusted Sour Cream Coffee Ring.

SOUR CREAM COFFEE RING

Baked in a bundt or other fancy tube pan, this wheaty coffee cake makes a dramatic presentation. As you cut each slice, you'll see a swirled layer of the spicy nut filling.

- 2 cups all-purpose flour
- 1 cup whole wheat flour
- ¾ teaspoon baking soda
- 1 tablespoon baking powder
- ½ teaspoon salt
- ¾ cup butter or margarine, softened
- 1 cup granulated sugar
- ½ cup firmly packed brown sugar
- 1 teaspoon vanilla extract
- 3 eggs
- 1½ cups sour cream
- 2 tablespoons cold butter or margarine, cut in pieces
  Confectioners' sugar

Cinnamon-Walnut Filling

- ½ cup sugar
- 1½ teaspoons ground cinnamon
- ½ cup finely chopped walnuts

1. Preheat oven to 350° F. In a medium bowl stir together flours, soda, baking powder, and salt.

2. In a large bowl cream the ¾ cup butter with sugars until light and fluffy. Blend in vanilla. Then add eggs, one at a time, beating well after each addition.

3. Add flour mixture to creamed mixture alternately with sour cream, mixing to blend after each addition.

4. Spoon about 2 tablespoons of the Cinnamon-Walnut Filling over bottom of a well-greased, lightly floured 10-inch bundt or other tube pan with a capacity of 10 to 12 cups. Spoon in half of the batter. Sprinkle evenly with about half of the remaining filling; dot with 1 tablespoon of the cold butter. Add remaining batter, then sprinkle with remaining filling, and dot with remaining butter.

5. Bake until cake tests done when a long skewer is inserted in thickest part (45 to 50 minutes).

6. Let stand in pan on a wire rack for about 10 minutes, then invert out of pan. Dust with confectioners' sugar before serving.

Makes 1 coffee cake.

Cinnamon-Walnut Filling In a small bowl mix sugar, cinnamon, and walnuts.

BLUEBERRY COFFEE CAKE

Dust confectioners' sugar over this almond-crusted fresh blueberry cake to dramatize its luscious looks.

- ¼ cup each *sliced almonds and firmly packed brown sugar*
- 1½ cups flour
- ¾ cup granulated sugar
- 1 tablespoon baking powder
- ½ teaspoon salt
- ¼ teaspoon ground nutmeg
- ⅓ cup butter
- 1 cup fresh blueberries
- 1 egg
- ½ cup milk
- 1 teaspoon vanilla extract
  Confectioners' sugar

1. Preheat oven to 350° F. Generously grease a 9-inch tube pan with a capacity of 6 to 7 cups. Sprinkle with mixture of almonds and brown sugar; set aside.

2. In a large bowl mix flour, granulated sugar, baking powder, salt, and nutmeg; cut in butter until mixture resembles coarse crumbs. Lightly stir in blueberries.

3. In a small bowl beat egg lightly with milk and vanilla. Stir milk mixture into blueberry mixture just until combined. Spread batter gently in prepared pan.

4. Bake until coffee cake is well browned and a long skewer inserted in thickest part comes out clean (45 minutes to 1 hour).

5. Let stand in pan for about 5 minutes, loosen edges, and invert onto a serving plate. Serve warm or at room temperature, dusted with confectioners' sugar.

Makes 1 coffee cake.

TOASTED-COCONUT BANANA BREAD

A generous measure of coconut lends a tropical flavor to this favorite fruit-nut bread.

> 1 cup *flaked coconut*
> 2 cups *flour*
> 1 tablespoon *baking powder*
> 1 teaspoon *ground cinnamon*
> ½ teaspoon each *salt and baking soda*
> ¾ cup *sugar*
> 1 cup *finely chopped walnuts*
> 1 *egg*
> ¼ cup *milk*
> ⅓ cup *salad oil*
> 1 teaspoon *vanilla extract*
> 2 *soft-ripe bananas*

1. Preheat oven to 350° F. Spread coconut in a shallow pan and bake, stirring occasionally, until lightly toasted (12 to 15 minutes). Set aside to cool.

2. In a large bowl mix flour, baking powder, cinnamon, salt, soda, and sugar. Stir in walnuts and coconut.

3. Beat egg with milk, oil, and vanilla until well combined. Mash bananas (you should have about 1 cup); blend with egg mixture. Add banana mixture to dry ingredients, mixing just until blended.

4. Spread in a greased, lightly floured 4½- by 8½-inch loaf pan.

5. Bake until loaf is well browned and a wooden toothpick inserted in center comes out clean (50 to 60 minutes). Let stand 10 minutes, then turn out onto a wire rack to cool completely. Flavor is best if, after cooling, bread is wrapped and allowed to stand at least 1 day.

Makes 1 loaf.

Served warm or at room temperature, almond-crusted Blueberry Coffee Cake is inviting for breakfast. Like many of the pastries in this chapter, it makes an excellent coffee-break snack as well.

CINNAMON COFFEE CAKE "PIE"

Vinegar adds a tang to the flavor of this old-time breakfast bread, sweetened, in part, with honey. Baked in an 8-inch round cake pan, the coffee cake is just the right size for a weekend morning treat.

  1½ cups flour
  ¾   teaspoon each baking soda and ground cinnamon
  ½   teaspoon salt
  ⅓   cup butter, softened
  ¼   cup sugar
  ½   cup honey
  1   teaspoon vanilla extract
  2   eggs
  3   tablespoons white vinegar

Confectioners' Sugar Topping

  2   tablespoons confectioners' sugar
  ½   teaspoon ground cinnamon

1. Preheat oven to 375° F. Stir together flour, soda, cinnamon, and salt.

2. In large bowl of electric mixer, cream butter and sugar until fluffy. Blend in honey and vanilla. Then add eggs, one at a time, beating well after each addition.

3. Add flour mixture to creamed mixture alternately with vinegar, mixing to blend after each addition. Spread batter in a greased, lightly floured 8-inch round cake pan. Sprinkle evenly with Confectioners' Sugar Topping.

4. Bake until wooden toothpick inserted in center comes out clean (25 to 30 minutes). Cut in wedges and serve warm.

Makes 1 coffee cake.

Confectioners' Sugar Topping
In a small bowl mix confectioners' sugar and cinnamon until well combined.

CARAMEL-TOPPED OATMEAL BREAKFAST CAKE

A broiled brown sugar and nut topping gilds this moist, spicy breakfast cake. It is delicious with tea.

  1¼ cups boiling water
  1   cup rolled oats
  ½   cup raisins
  ½   cup butter, softened
  1   cup granulated sugar
  1   cup firmly packed brown sugar
  1   teaspoon vanilla extract
  2   eggs
  1½ cups flour
  1   teaspoon baking soda
  ¾   teaspoon ground cinnamon
  ½   teaspoon salt
  ¼   teaspoon ground nutmeg

Caramel Topping

  ¼   cup butter or margarine
  ½   cup firmly packed brown sugar
  2   tablespoons half-and-half
  1   cup finely chopped walnuts

1. Preheat oven to 350° F. Pour boiling water over oats and raisins in a medium bowl; let stand until warm.

2. In large bowl of electric mixer, cream butter with sugars until light and fluffy. Blend in vanilla. Then add eggs, one at a time, beating well after each addition. Blend in oatmeal mixture.

3. Stir together flour, soda, cinnamon, salt, and nutmeg. Blend flour mixture into oatmeal mixture. Spread batter in a well-greased, lightly floured 9-inch square baking pan.

4. Bake until top of cake springs back (45 to 50 minutes).

5. Spread lightly with Caramel Topping. Broil, about 4 inches from heat, until topping browns and bubbles (about 2 minutes). Let cool slightly, then cut into squares.

Serves 10 to 12.

Caramel Topping In a small pan melt butter. Remove from heat and mix in brown sugar, half-and-half, and walnuts.

YEAST BREADS

Breads leavened with yeast take more time, work, and attention than do quick breads. But for those who enjoy creating—and eating—such breads, the rewards surpass the effort. Here is a sampling of yeast breads with special morning appeal.

EASY BATTER BRIOCHES

Here are eggy, golden rolls to complement almost any brunch main dish—or to serve simply with butter and jam.

  2   packages active dry yeast
  ¼   cup warm water
  ½   cup warm milk
  ⅔   cup butter
  ¼   cup sugar
  ½   teaspoon salt
  3¾ to 4 cups flour
  4   eggs

1. Sprinkle yeast over water in large bowl of electric mixer. Let stand until soft (about 5 minutes). Add milk, butter, sugar, and salt; stir until butter melts.

2. Blend in 2 cups of the flour; beat at medium speed for 3 minutes. Add eggs, one at a time, beating well after each addition. Gradually beat in 1¾ to 2 cups additional flour to make a stiff batter, beating until batter is smooth (3 to 5 minutes).

3. Transfer batter to a greased bowl, cover, and let rise in a warm place until bubbly (about 1 hour). Stir batter down, then fill well-greased 2½-inch muffin pans about two-thirds full.

4. Let rise until doubled (20 to 25 minutes).

5. Preheat oven to 350° F. Bake until well browned (20 to 25 minutes). Let stand in pans for a few minutes, then remove to wire racks to cool.

Makes 18 rolls.

ORANGE BATTER BREAD

Beating the batter until it is so elastic that it pulls away from the side of the bowl is important for this yeast bread.

    2 packages active dry yeast
    ¼ cup warm water
    ½ cup warm milk
    ⅓ cup sugar
    ¾ teaspoon salt
    ⅔ cup butter, softened
    1½ teaspoons vanilla extract
    4 eggs
    1 teaspoon grated orange rind
    4 cups flour
       Chopped toasted almonds,
       for garnish

Orange Glaze

    1 cup confectioners' sugar
    2 teaspoons butter, softened
    ½ teaspoon grated orange rind
    2 tablespoons orange juice

1. Sprinkle yeast over water in large bowl of electric mixer; let stand until soft (about 5 minutes). Add milk, sugar, salt, and butter; stir until butter melts. Mix in vanilla, eggs, and orange rind, beating until well combined.

2. Add flour, 1 cup at a time, beating well after each addition. When all the flour has been added, beat at medium speed until batter is elastic (3 to 5 minutes).

3. Transfer batter to a greased bowl. Cover and let rise in a warm place until bubbly (about 1 hour). Stir down; spread batter in a well-greased 10-inch tube pan, bundt pan, or other fancy 10- to 12-cup mold. Let rise until doubled (about 45 minutes).

4. Preheat oven to 350° F. Bake until well browned (30 to 35 minutes).

5. Invert bread from pan onto a wire rack to cool. While still warm, drizzle with Orange Glaze and decorate with almonds.

Makes 1 large coffee cake.

Orange Glaze In a small bowl combine confectioners' sugar, butter, orange rind, and orange juice. Mix until smooth.

BRAIDED EGG BREAD

Nothing exceeds this traditional *challah*. The crust is speckled with sesame or poppy seeds.

    1 package active dry yeast
    1¼ cups warm water
    2 teaspoons sugar
    1 teaspoon salt
    2 tablespoons salad oil
    4½ to 5 cups flour
    2 eggs
    1 egg yolk, beaten with
       ½ teaspoon water
    3 tablespoons sesame seed
       or poppy seed

1. Sprinkle yeast over ¼ cup of the water in large bowl of electric mixer. Let stand until soft (about 5 minutes). Add remaining 1 cup water, sugar, salt, and oil.

2. Add 3 cups of the flour. Mix to blend, then beat at medium speed until smooth and elastic (about 5 minutes). Beat in eggs, one at a time, then gradually stir in about 1½ cups more of the flour to make a soft dough.

3. Turn dough out onto a board or pastry cloth coated with some of the remaining ½ cup flour. Knead until dough is smooth and satiny and small bubbles form just under surface, adding more flour to prevent dough from being too sticky (about 15 minutes).

4. Transfer dough to a greased bowl. Cover and let rise in a warm place until doubled (about 1 hour). Punch down, cover again, and let rise a second time until doubled (about 45 minutes). Punch down and divide into 3 equal portions.

5. On a lightly floured surface, roll each portion to an 18-inch-long strand. Place the 3 strands side by side diagonally across a greased baking sheet; braid. Pinch ends to seal. Let rise until almost doubled (about 45 minutes). Preheat oven to 375° F. Brush egg yolk mixture lightly over braid. Sprinkle evenly with sesame or poppy seed.

6. Bake until braid is well browned and sounds hollow when tapped lightly (40 to 45 minutes).

Makes 1 large loaf.

HONEY-WHEAT TOASTING BREAD

If peanut butter with toast is your idea of a wonderful morning combination, try it on this bread for breakfast. The dense, intensely flavorful bread is also fine with homemade preserves.

    2 packages active dry yeast
    ½ cup warm water
    2 cups warm milk
    ½ cup honey
    2 tablespoons salad oil
    2 teaspoons salt
    3 cups whole wheat flour
    3½ to 4 cups all-purpose flour
    1 cup wheat germ

1. Sprinkle yeast over water in large bowl of an electric mixer; let stand until soft (about 5 minutes). Stir in milk, honey, oil, salt, whole wheat flour, and 2 cups of the all-purpose flour. Mix to blend, then beat at medium speed until smooth and elastic (about 5 minutes).

2. Mix in wheat germ and about 1½ cups of the all-purpose flour to make a moderately stiff dough. Turn out on a board or pastry cloth floured with some of the remaining ½ cup all-purpose flour. Knead until dough is elastic and small bubbles form just beneath surface (about 10 minutes).

3. Transfer dough to a greased bowl. Cover and let rise in a warm place until doubled (1 to 1½ hours). Punch dough down, divide into two equal parts, and let rest 10 minutes. Shape into two loaves and place in greased 4½- by 8½-inch baking pans. Cover and let rise until loaves fill pans to tops (30 to 45 minutes).

4. Preheat oven to 375° F. Bake until loaves are well browned and sound hollow when tapped (30 to 35 minutes). Turn out onto racks to cool before slicing and toasting.

Makes 2 loaves.

ITALIAN SAUSAGE BREAD

Crumbled sausage flavors this round, wheat-flecked loaf, a specialty of Italian bakers in New Jersey.

- 1 package active dry yeast
- ¼ cup warm water
- 1 cup warm milk
- 1 tablespoon sugar
- ½ teaspoon salt
- 2 tablespoons olive oil
- 3 to 3¼ cups all-purpose flour
- ½ cup whole wheat flour
- ½ pound mild Italian sausages
- 1 egg yolk, beaten with 1 teaspoon water

1. Sprinkle yeast over water in large bowl of electric mixer. Let stand until soft (about 5 minutes). Stir in milk, sugar, salt, and 1 tablespoon of the olive oil.

2. Add 2½ cups of the all-purpose flour. Mix to blend, then beat at medium speed until smooth and elastic (about 5 minutes). Stir in whole wheat flour and about ¼ cup more all-purpose flour to make a stiff dough.

3. Turn dough out onto a board or pastry cloth coated with some of the remaining ¼ to ½ cup all-purpose flour. Knead until dough is smooth and satiny and small bubbles form just under surface, adding more all-purpose flour to prevent dough from being too sticky (about 15 minutes).

4. Transfer dough to a greased bowl. Cover and let rise in a warm place until doubled (45 minutes to 1 hour). Meanwhile, remove casings from sausages and crumble meat. In a medium frying pan over moderate heat, brown lightly, stirring often. Remove with a slotted spoon and drain and cool on paper towels. Punch dough down and pat into a ½-inch-thick circle.

5. Sprinkle sausage over round of dough. Knead and fold lightly into dough, then shape it into a ball. Pat out to a round 8 inches in diameter. Place on a greased baking sheet. With a 3¼-inch round cutter or empty tuna can, cut a circle in center, leaving round of dough in place.

6. Brush dough with remaining 1 tablespoon olive oil. Let rise until light and puffy. Brush with egg yolk mixture.

7. Preheat oven to 375° F. Bake until crust is a rich golden brown and loaf sounds hollow when tapped (25 to 30 minutes). Cool slightly on a rack before slicing. Cut in wedges to serve.

Makes 1 large loaf.

FILBERT LOAVES

Toasted filberts—some call them hazelnuts—perfume these rich, sweet little loaves. The bread is delicious spread with the rich, creamy Italian cheese called mascarpone.

This recipe makes two small loaves, so you can serve one now and freeze the other. You can also bake the bread in a single 5- by 9-inch loaf pan, allowing longer for the larger loaf to rise and bake.

- ¾ cup filberts
- 1 package active dry yeast
- ¼ cup warm water
- ½ cup warm milk
- ¼ cup sugar
- ½ teaspoon each salt, vanilla extract, and grated lemon rind
- 2 tablespoons butter or margarine
- 3 to 3¼ cups flour
- 2 eggs
- 1 teaspoon water
- 1 tablespoon sugar

1. Preheat oven to 350° F. Spread filberts in a shallow pan. Bake until lightly browned (8 to 10 minutes). Cool slightly, then chop coarsely.

2. Sprinkle yeast over water in large bowl of electric mixer. Let stand until soft (about 5 minutes). Add milk, the ¼ cup sugar, salt, vanilla, lemon rind, and butter. Stir until butter melts.

3. Add 1½ cups of the flour. Mix to blend, then beat at medium speed until smooth and elastic (about 5 minutes). Beat in 1 whole egg and egg yolk (reserve egg white for glaze), then ½ cup of the filberts. Gradually stir in about 1¼ cups more flour to make a soft dough.

4. Turn dough out onto a board or pastry cloth coated with some of the remaining ¼ to ½ cup flour. Knead until dough is smooth and satiny and small bubbles form just under surface, adding more flour to prevent dough from being too sticky (about 15 minutes).

5. Transfer dough to a greased bowl. Cover and let rise in a warm place until doubled (1¼ to 1½ hours). Punch dough down and divide it into 2 equal portions.

6. Sprinkle 2 greased small loaf pans (about 3½ by 7½ inches) lightly with some of the remaining chopped filberts, using about 1 tablespoon for each pan. Shape each half of dough into a loaf. Place in prepared pans. Let rise until almost doubled (about 45 minutes). Preheat oven to 375° F. Slightly beat reserved egg white with the 1 teaspoon water; brush mixture lightly over loaves. Sprinkle with remaining filberts and the 1 tablespoon sugar. (Use 1½ teaspoons sugar for each loaf.)

7. Bake until well browned (25 to 30 minutes).

Makes 2 small loaves.

CROISSANTS

Crisp, flaky, butter in every crumb—croissants are the essence of the Continental breakfast. More and more bakers are turning out croissants that rival those made in France. If you are willing to spend the time, so can you.

This is one recipe that calls for butter and butter alone; margarine just doesn't produce the same flavor or crisply layered texture. If you are going to take the trouble to make croissants, it is worth using the best ingredients.

  1 package active dry yeast
  ¼ cup warm water
  ¾ cup warm milk
  1 tablespoon sugar
  ¼ teaspoon salt
  1 tablespoon butter, softened
  2¾ cups flour
  1 cup butter, softened
  1 egg yolk, beaten with 1
    teaspoon water

1. Sprinkle yeast over water in large bowl of electric mixer. Let stand until soft (about 5 minutes). Add milk, sugar, salt, and the 1 tablespoon butter, stirring until butter melts.

2. Add 1¼ cups of the flour. Mix to blend, then beat at medium speed until smooth (about 3 minutes). Mix in about 1 cup more of the flour to make a soft dough.

3. Turn out on board or pastry cloth floured with the remaining ½ cup flour. Turn dough in flour to coat well. Knead gently until flour is incorporated.

4. Transfer dough to greased bowl. Cover and let rise in a warm place until doubled (45 minutes to 1 hour). Punch down, cover, and refrigerate for at least 1 hour (or as long as several hours or overnight).

5. Roll dough out to a rectangle about ¼ inch thick. Using a fourth of the 1 cup butter (it should be just soft enough to spread, but not melting), spread it over the center third of the dough.

6. Fold sides of dough over buttered center, sealing edges. Again roll dough out to a ¼-inch-thick rectangle. Spread center third with another fourth of the butter, then repeat folding and sealing. Wrap dough in plastic wrap and refrigerate for 30 minutes.

7. Again roll dough to a ¼-inch-thick rectangle, spread with another fourth of the butter, fold, and seal. If dough is soft, wrap and refrigerate for another 30 minutes; otherwise, continue. Then complete dough by rolling to a ¼-inch-thick rectangle, spreading center third with last fourth of the butter, and folding and sealing as before. Wrap again and refrigerate until firm (1 hour or longer).

8. Divide dough in half. (Wrap and return half to refrigerator.) Roll each portion of dough out on floured surface to a 13-inch-diameter circle. Cut each circle into 6 equal triangles. Starting from wide end of each, roll toward point. Place each roll with point on underside on ungreased baking sheet, curving ends to make a crescent shape.

9. Cover lightly with plastic wrap and let rise at room temperature until nearly doubled (45 minutes to 1 hour). Preheat oven to 400° F. Brush lightly with egg yolk mixture.

10. Bake for 10 minutes; reduce heat to 350° F and bake until croissants are golden brown (18 to 20 minutes).

Makes 1 dozen rolls.

HOW TO MAKE CROISSANTS

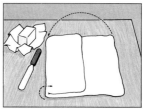

1. Roll chilled dough out to a rectangle, then spread ¼ cup softened butter over center third of it.

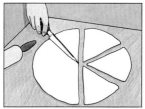

2. Fold outside thirds of the dough from both sides over buttered center. Seal edges, then chill dough. Repeat rolling, buttering, and folding steps three more times until all the butter is incorporated.

3. Divide dough in half and refrigerate until firm. Roll each half out to a 13-inch-diameter circle, then cut into 6 equal triangles.

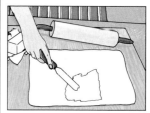

4. Starting from wide end, roll each triangle of dough gently but firmly toward point. Curve into a crescent; place on baking sheet with points underneath.

CINNAMON-RAISIN BUNS

Wheat germ in the dough gives these coiled raisin rolls a nutlike flavor.

 2 packages active dry yeast
 1¾ cups warm water
 ⅓ cup sugar
 1 teaspoon salt
 3 tablespoons salad oil
 4½ to 5 cups flour
 ⅓ cup wheat germ
 ⅓ cup cold butter or margarine, thinly sliced
 ½ cup raisins

Cinnamon-Sugar

 ½ cup sugar
 1 tablespoon ground cinnamon

Egg White Glaze

 1 egg white
 1 teaspoon water
 ½ teaspoon sugar

Confectioners' Sugar Frosting

 ¾ cup confectioners' sugar
 ½ teaspoon vanilla extract
 1½ to 2 tablespoons warm water

1. In large bowl of electric mixer, sprinkle yeast over water; let stand until softened (about 5 minutes). Mix in sugar, salt, and oil. Stir in 3 cups of the flour, then beat at medium speed until mixture is elastic and pulls away from sides of bowl (about 5 minutes).

2. Stir in wheat germ and about 1½ cups more of the flour to make a soft dough. Turn out on a board or pastry cloth coated with some of the remaining ½ cup flour. Knead until dough is smooth and satiny and small bubbles form beneath surface, kneading in additional flour as needed if dough seems sticky (15 to 20 minutes).

3. Place dough in a greased bowl, turning to coat all sides. Cover and let rise in warm place until doubled in bulk (about 1 hour).

4. Punch dough down. Roll out on a floured surface to a 12- by 18-inch rectangle. Cover evenly with butter slices, then sprinkle with Cinnamon-Sugar. Sprinkle evenly with raisins. Starting from a long end, roll dough up, jelly-roll fashion. Moisten and pinch edge to seal. Cut into 12 equal slices.

5. Place slices, cut sides down, in a well-greased 10- by 15-inch baking pan. Cover with waxed paper and let rise until rolls are puffy (25 to 30 minutes). Preheat oven to 400° F. Brush rolls with Egg White Glaze.

6. Bake until well browned (20 to 25 minutes). Serve warm or at room temperature, drizzled with Confectioners' Sugar Frosting.

Makes 1 dozen rolls.

Cinnamon-Sugar In a small bowl mix sugar and cinnamon.

Egg White Glaze In a small bowl beat egg white with water and sugar until slightly foamy.

Confectioners' Sugar Frosting Place confectioners' sugar in a small bowl. Add vanilla and warm water, mixing until smooth and creamy.

BAKED NUTMEG DOUGHNUTS

Although these doughnut-shaped rolls are baked, not fried, they resemble a doughnut in flavor. The dough requires no kneading and is light and puffy in texture.

 2 packages active dry yeast
 ¼ cup warm water
 1⅓ cups warm milk
 ¼ cup sugar
 1 teaspoon salt
 2 teaspoons ground nutmeg
 ¼ teaspoon ground cinnamon
 ⅔ cup butter
 4½ to 5 cups flour
 2 eggs
 ½ cup Vanilla Sugar (see page 30)

1. Sprinkle yeast over water in large bowl of electric mixer. Let stand until soft (about 5 minutes). Add milk, the ¼ cup sugar, salt, nutmeg, cinnamon, and ⅓ cup of the butter; stir until butter melts.

2. Add 3 cups of the flour. Mix to blend, then beat at medium speed until smooth and elastic (about 5 minutes). Beat in eggs, then gradually stir in about 1½ cups more of the flour to make a soft dough.

3. Transfer to a greased bowl, cover, and let rise in a warm place until doubled (about 1 hour). Stir the dough down.

4. Turn dough out on a well-floured board or pastry cloth (use some of the remaining ½ cup flour) and shape with floured hands into a flattened ball; coat well with flour. Lightly roll out about ½ inch thick. Cut with a floured 2½-inch doughnut cutter. Place doughnuts about 2 inches apart on greased baking sheets.

5. Brush lightly with some of the remaining ⅓ cup butter, melted, and let rise until nearly doubled (about 30 minutes).

6. Preheat oven to 425° F. Bake until doughnuts are golden brown (about 10 minutes). Brush warm doughnuts with remaining melted butter and roll lightly in Vanilla Sugar.

Makes 3 dozen doughnuts.

menu

SWISS CHRISTMAS BREAKFAST

Oranges

Swiss Almond Fruit Loaves

Butter

Soft-Cooked Eggs

Hot Chocolate or Coffee

Here is a holiday-morning breakfast to enjoy in stages. Amid the excitement of emptying the Christmas stockings and unwrapping the packages beneath the tree, munch orange sections and sip chocolate or coffee.

Wrap the previously baked loaves in foil and put them in the oven to warm, then cook eggs when the hubbub subsides. (They take only three to five minutes; see page 41.)

SWISS ALMOND FRUIT LOAVES

> 2 *packages active dry yeast*
> ½ *cup warm water*
> 1 *cup warm milk*
> ¼ *cup butter, softened*
> ¼ *cup sugar*
> 1 *teaspoon each salt and ground mace or nutmeg*
> 4½ *to 5 cups flour*
> 1 *egg*
> ½ *cup each raisins, slivered almonds, and diced mixed candied fruits*
> 2 *tablespoons egg white, slightly beaten*
> 2 *tablespoons Vanilla Sugar (see page 30)*

1. Sprinkle yeast over water in large bowl of electric mixer. Let stand until soft (about 5 minutes). Add milk, butter, sugar, salt, and mace; stir until butter melts.

2. Add 3 cups of the flour. Mix to blend, then beat until smooth and elastic (about 5 minutes). Beat in egg. Stir in about 1 cup more of the flour to make a soft dough. Mix in raisins, almonds, and fruits.

3. Turn dough out on a board or pastry cloth coated with some of the remaining ½ to 1 cup flour; knead until dough is smooth, springy, and small bubbles form just under the surface (15 to 20 minutes).

4. Transfer dough to a greased bowl. Cover and let rise in a warm place until doubled (about 1 hour). Punch dough down. Turn out on a floured surface and knead lightly to expel air bubbles. Divide into 2 equal parts.

5. Shape each half of the dough into a loaf. Place in generously greased 4½- by 8½-inch loaf pans.

6. Let rise until dough just reaches tops of pans (30 to 45 minutes). Preheat oven to 375° F. Brush tops of loaves lightly with beaten egg white. Sprinkle evenly with Vanilla Sugar.

7. Bake until loaves are well browned and sound hollow when tapped (30 to 35 minutes). Carefully remove from pans and let cool on wire racks.

Makes 2 loaves.

123

HONEY-NUT CRESCENTS

Rolled from wedges of sour cream dough into small crescents, these fruit-filled tidbits (some call them *rugalach*) are something of a breakfast cookie.

  1 package active dry yeast
  ¼ cup warm water
  2½ cups flour
  ½ teaspoon salt
  ½ cup butter or margarine
  2 eggs, separated
  ½ teaspoon vanilla extract
  ½ cup sour cream
   Confectioners' sugar
  ¼ cup honey
  ½ cup raisins
  ⅔ cup chopped walnuts
  ¼ cup granulated sugar, mixed
   with ½ teaspoon ground
   cinnamon
  2 teaspoons water

1. In a medium bowl sprinkle yeast over the ¼ cup water and let stand until soft (about 5 minutes).

2. In large bowl of electric mixer, stir together flour and salt. Cut in butter until mixture resembles coarse crumbs. To yeast mixture add egg yolks (reserve whites for glaze), vanilla, and sour cream; beat until blended. Gradually add yeast mixture to flour mixture, mixing until flour is moistened. Turn dough out onto a floured board or pastry cloth and knead just until smooth; shape dough into a flattened ball.

3. Wrap dough in plastic wrap and refrigerate for several hours or overnight.

4. Divide dough in half. Roll each half out to a 12-inch-diameter circle on board or pastry cloth sprinkled lightly with confectioners' sugar. Warm honey slightly to make it easier to spread. Brush each round of dough with half of the honey, then sprinkle with half each of the raisins, walnuts, and cinnamon-sugar mixture.

5. Cut each round into 12 equal triangles. Starting at the wide end, roll each wedge toward point. Place, points down, about 2 inches apart on greased baking sheets. Curve ends slightly to make a crescent shape.

6. Cover crescents lightly with waxed paper and let stand in a warm place until puffy looking (20 to 25 minutes). Preheat oven to 350° F. Beat reserved egg whites with the 2 teaspoons water. Brush crescents lightly with egg white mixture.

7. Bake until rolls are richly browned (18 to 20 minutes).

Makes 2 dozen rolls.

ITALIAN JAM-FILLED CRESCENTS

Although they are shaped like crescents, these rolls have a much more tender, briochelike texture than flaky French croissants. Each reveals a center of apricot preserves.

  2 packages active dry yeast
  ½ cup warm water
  ¾ cup warm milk
  ¾ cup granulated sugar
  1 teaspoon each *salt and
   vanilla extract*
  ½ cup butter or margarine,
   softened
  5½ to 6 cups flour
  3 eggs
  ½ cup apricot preserves or
   orange marmalade
  2 teaspoons water
   Pearl sugar or coarsely
   crushed sugar cubes

1. Sprinkle yeast over water in large bowl of electric mixer. Let stand until soft (about 5 minutes). Add milk, granulated sugar, salt, vanilla, and butter; stir until butter melts.

2. Add 3 cups of the flour. Mix to blend, then beat at medium speed until smooth and elastic (about 5 minutes). Beat in 1 whole egg and 2 egg yolks (reserve 2 egg whites for glaze). Gradually stir in 2 to 2½ cups more flour to make a soft dough.

3. Turn dough out onto a board or pastry cloth coated with some of the remaining ½ to 1 cup flour. Knead until dough is smooth and satiny and small bubbles form just under surface, adding more flour to prevent dough from being too sticky (about 15 minutes).

4. Turn dough in a greased bowl. Cover and let rise in a warm place until doubled (about 1½ hours). Punch dough down, divide it into 2 equal portions, and let stand for 10 minutes.

5. Roll each portion of dough out on a floured surface to an 18-inch-diameter circle. Cut each round into 12 equal triangles. Place about 1 teaspoon preserves at wide end of each triangle. Starting from wide end of each, roll toward point. Place each roll on a greased baking sheet with point on underside, curving ends slightly to make a crescent shape.

6. Cover lightly and let rolls rise until puffy looking (25 to 30 minutes). Preheat oven to 375° F. Beat reserved 2 egg whites with the 2 teaspoons water. Brush egg white mixture lightly over rolls. Sprinkle lightly with pearl sugar.

7. Bake until well browned (15 to 20 minutes).

Makes 2 dozen rolls.

*This brunch menu features
Scrambled Eggs in Crisp Crust,
Four Seasons Fresh Fruit,
Spiced Cranberry Muffins, and
Italian Jam-Filled Crescents.*

INDEX

Note: Page numbers in italics refer to illustrations separated from recipe text.

A

Almond Dessert Crêpes, 92
Almond Fruit Loaves, 123
Almond Press-In Pastry, 109
Apple Cider, Hot Spiced, *20, 21*
Apple(s)
  Calvados Soufflé, 60
  Chicken and Spiced Apple Crêpes, 86
  Chunky Sautéed Apples with Lemon, 32, *34*
  Cinnamon-Pink Applesauce, 32
  Italian Baked Apples with Prunes, *33, 34*
  Maple Apple Crisp, 32
  Nutty Baked, 34
  -Pecan Muffins, 113
  Puffy Apple Fritters, 37
  Shredded Apple Cake, 73
Apricot Tart, 109
Artichoke and Onion Frittata, 55
Asparagus and Mushroom Crêpes, 90
Asparagus and Seafood Quiche, 101
Avocado and Shrimp Omelet, 52

B

Bacon
  Hangtown Fry, 78, *79*
  Sweet Corn and Bacon Quiche, 106, *107*
Banana Bread, Toasted-Coconut, 117
Banana Daiquiri, 24
Banana Hotcakes with Honey-Pecan Butter, 83
Banana Lemon Drink, 19
Banana-Nut Coffee Cake, *20,* 115
Beans, Refried, 42
Belgian waffle iron, 85
Belgian Waffles with Blueberry Sauce, 96
Bellini, *22,* 24
Berries Romanoff, 36
Beverages, 8, 12–25
  alcoholic, 16, 22–25, *46*
  Banana Daiquiri, 24
  Banana-Lemon Drink, 19
  Bellini, *22,* 24
  blender drinks, 19, 21
  Bloody Mary, 25
  Breakfast-in-a-Glass, 19
  coffee, 12, 13–16
  fruit juices, 8, 12, 21–22
  Hazel's Ramos Gin Fizz, 23, *46*
  hot chocolate drinks, *17,* 18
  Hot Mulled Cranberry Punch, 22
  Hot Spiced Cider, *20, 21*
  Irish Coffee, 16
  Mimosa, 23
  Nectarine-Plum Drink, 19
  Orange Spiced Tea, 18
  Piña Colada, *23,* 24
  Pink Fruit Juice Froth, 21
  Sangria, 25
  Spirited Milk Punch, 24
  Strawberry Daiquiri, *23,* 24
  Strawberry Drink, 19
  tea, 18
  Tequila Sunrise, *23,* 24
  wines, 22, 24, 25
  Winter Citrus Wake-Up, 21
Biscuits
  Breakfast Strawberry Shortcake, 35
  Ham Pinwheel, 41
Blackberry Cobbler, 36–37

Blender drinks. *See* Beverages
Blini, 81
  pan for, 85
  Quick Buckwheat, 84
Blintzes, 81
  Buttermilk, 92–93
  Strawberry Blintz Omelets, 53
Bloody Mary, 25
Blueberries
  Belgian Waffles with Blueberry Sauce, 96
  Blueberry Coffee Cake, 116–17
  Blueberry Yogurt Pancakes, 82
  and Peaches with Cream, 31
Blue Cheese Quiche, 103
Braided Egg Bread (*Challah*), *56, 110,* 119
Breads, quick, 111, 112–14
  See also Cake; Muffins
  Auntie's Scones, 114
  Crisp Popovers, 115
  Toasted-Coconut Banana Bread, 117
Breads, yeast, 111, 118–20
  See also Brioche(s); Croissants; Rolls
  Braided Egg Bread (*Challah*), *56, 110,* 119
  Filbert Loaves, *110,* 120
  Honey-Wheat Toasting Bread, *110,* 119
  Italian Sausage Bread, *110,* 120
  Orange Batter Bread, 119
  Swiss Almond Fruit Loaves, 123
Breakfast in Bed, 97
Breton Seafood Crêpes, 88
Breton-Style Sausage and Spinach Crêpes, 88, *89*
Brie and Ham Omelet, 52
Brioche(s)
  Chicken Tarragon-Filled, 70
  Easy Batter, 118
  Hot Pork and Ham Pâté in, 108
British-style breakfasts, 6
  Broiled Kippers with Sweet-Sour Onions, 75
  Kedgeree, 74
  Toad-in-the-Hole, 94
Buckwheat Blini, 84
Buckwheat Crêpes, 88
Buns
  Cinnamon-Raisin, 122
  Nippy Egg and Cheese, 42
  Ham-Filled Rye Buns with Mustard Sauce, 72, *73*
Buttermilk Blintzes, 92–93
Butter
  Honey, 114
  Honey-Pecan, 83
  Orange, 92

C

Café au Lait, 16
Caffè Latté, 16
Cake
  Banana Nut Coffee Cake, *20,* 115
  Blueberry Coffee Cake, 116–17
  Breakfast Strawberry Shortcake, 35
  Caramel-Topped Oatmeal Breakfast Cake, 118
  Cinnamon Coffee Cake "Pie," 118
  Lemon Drop Teacake, 115
  Shredded-Apple, 73
  Sour Cream Coffee Ring, 116
Calvados Custard Sauce, 60
Calvados Soufflé, 60
Cantaloupe, 8, 31
Cereal, ready-to-eat, 6
Challah (Braided Egg Bread), *56, 110,* 119

Champagne, 22, 23
Cheese
  Blue Cheese Quiche, 103
  Brie and Ham Omelet, 52
  Buttermilk Blintzes, 93
  Cheddar Cheese Muffins, *10–11,* 113
  Four Cheeses Soufflé, 57
  Grilled Cheese-and-Tomato Sandwiches, 95
  Ham and Cheese Custard Pie, 103
  Nippy Cheese Sauce, 67
  Nippy Egg and Cheese Buns, 42
  Parmesan Baked Eggs, *56,* 57
  Sherried Swiss Cheese Sauce, 45
  -Speckled Eggs, 44
  -Stuffed Baked Green Chiles, 58
  Truffled Ham and Cheese Crêpes, 91
Chicken
  Mexican Chicken and Chile Crêpes, 86–87
  Maple Baked, 71
  Pot Pie, 102–3
  and Spiced Apple Crêpes, 86
  Tarragon-Filled Brioches, 70
  and Veal Filo Rolls, 104–5
  Yankee Clipper, 69
Chicken Livers, Poached Eggs with, 45
Chiles
  Cheese-Stuffed Baked Green, 58
  Mexican Chicken and Chile Crêpes, 86–87
Chocolate-Almond Cookie Bark, *46, 47*
Chocolate drinks, *17,* 18
Christmas breakfast menu, 123
Cider, Hot Spiced, *20, 21*
Cinnamon Coffee Cake "Pie," 118
Cinnamon Muffins, Miniature, 112
Cinnamon-Pink Applesauce, 32
Cinnamon-Raisin Buns, 122
Cinnamon-Sugar, 112
Citrus fruit
  Broiled Pink Grapefruit, 30
  Four Seasons Fresh Fruit Bowl, 30
  as vitamin C source, 8, 27
  Winter Citrus Wake-Up, 21
Coconut Banana Bread, 117
Coffee, 13, 14–16
Coffee cake. *See* Cake
Continental breakfast, 6
Cookies
  Chocolate-Almond Cookie Bark, *46,* 47
  Honey-Nut Crescents (*Rugalach*), 124
Corn
  Fritters, 97
  Sweet Corn and Bacon Quiche, 106, *107*
Corned Beef Hash, Dilled, 67
Cornmeal Crêpes, 86, 87
Cornmeal pastries, 103, 106
Cottage Fried Potatoes, 66
Crab, in Asparagus and Seafood Quiche, 101
Cranberry Muffins, 113
Cranberry Punch, Hot Mulled, 22
Croissants, *16,* 121
Croque monsieur iron, 85, 95
Crêpe pan, 85
Crêpes, 81, 84–93
  Almond Dessert, 92
  Asparagus and Mushroom, 90
  basic, 84, 87
  Breton Seafood, 88
  Breton-Style Sausage and Spinach, 88, *89*
  Buckwheat, 88

Chicken and Spiced Apple, 86
  dessert, *89,* 92
  making and filling, 87
  Moussaka-Style Lamb, 87
  Orange-Buttered, *89,* 92
  Truffled Ham and Cheese, 91
  Whole Wheat, 87
Curried rice, in Kedgeree, 74
Curried Vegetable Omelets, 53
Curry Sauce, 71
Custard Sauce
  Calvados, 60
  for Moussaka-Style Lamb Crêpes, 87

D

Daiquiri, Banana, 24
Daiquiri, Strawberry, *23,* 24
Dessert crêpes, *89,* 92
Doughnuts, Baked Nutmeg, 122
Dressing, Russian, 105

E

Eggs, 38–61
  See also Frittata(s); Omelet(s); Soufflé(s)
  baked, 55–57
    Artichoke and Onion Frittata, 55
    Parmesan, *56,* 57
    Prosciutto, 57
    Swiss, 56
    in Tomato Sauce, 55
  Benedict, *46,* 47
  in blender drinks, 19
  cooked in the shell, *40,* 41–42
  fried, 42
    Cheese-Speckled, 44
    Fried Egg Muffin Sandwiches, 44
    with Tomato Sauce Mexicana (*huevos rancheros*), 42, *43*
  Hangtown Fry, 78, *79*
  hard-cooked, 41
    Egg and Broccoli Casserole with Ham Pinwheel Biscuits, 41
    Nippy Egg and Cheese Buns, 42
  Joe's Special, *62,* 64
  Nippy Egg and Cheese Buns, 42
  poached, 44, 45
    in Baked Potatoes, 48
    with Chicken Livers, 45
    Eggs Benedict, *46,* 47
    with Leeks, 48
    with Sorrel, 44–45
    Roulade with Mushroom Filling, 60, *61*
  scrambled, 49–50
    Calico, 49
    in a Crisp Crust, 50, *125*
    Italian Egg and Vegetable Scramble, 49
    Joe's Special, *62,* 64
  soft-cooked, *40,* 41
  shrimp-crowned, 41
Eggs Benedict Brunch for Eight, *46,* 47
English muffins
  Fried Egg Muffin Sandwiches, 44
  Nippy Egg and Cheese Buns, 42

F

Fall Family Breakfast, 37
Filbert Loaves, *110,* 120
Filo-wrapped pastries, 104–5
Finnan haddie, 74
Fish and shellfish, 74–79
  Asparagus and Seafood Quiche, 101
  Baked Stuffed Trout, *76,* 77
  Breton Seafood Crêpes, 88
  Broiled Kippers with Sweet-Sour Onions, 75

Crusty Oyster Gratin, 75
Fisherman's Pie, 78
Fresh Salmon Quiche, 103
Hangtown Fry, 78, *79*
Kedgeree, 74
Lobster Pie, 77
Scallops in Tomato Cream, 75
Shad Roe with Caper Butter, 77
French-style breakfasts, 6
Breton Seafood Crêpes, 88
Breton-Style Sausage and Spinach
Crêpes, 88, *89*
Orange-Buttered Dessert Crêpes, *89*,
92
Provençal Tomato Galettes, 108
French toast, 81, 95
Jam-Filled, 95
Monte Cristo Sandwich, 95
with Strawberries, 97
Frittata(s), 54–55
Baked Artichoke and Onion, 55
Country Vegetable, 54
Hangtown Fry, 78, *79*
Tomato, 55
Fritters
Puffy Apple, 37
Puffy Corn, 97
Fruit drinks, 19, 20, 21
Fruits, 26–37
See also specific fruits
Four Seasons Fresh Fruit Bowl,
28–29, 30, *125*
as vitamin C source, 8
Winter Fruit Compote, 32
Fruit tarts, 109
Frying pans, 8–9

G
Germany, breakfast foods in, 6
Gin Fizz, Hazel's Ramos, 23
Gingerbread Pancakes with Lemon
Sauce, 83
Grapefruit, Broiled Pink, 30

H
Haddock, smoked, 74
Ham
Brie and Ham Omelet, 52
and Cheese Custard Pie, 103
Ground Ham Filling, 72
Hot Pork and Ham Pâté in Brioche,
108
Karen's Ham and Spinach Rolls, 67
Monte Cristo Sandwich, 95
Pinwheel Biscuits, 41
Prosciutto Baked Eggs, 57
Provençal Tomato Galettes, 108
in Rye Buns with Mustard Sauce, 72,
73
Truffled Ham and Cheese Crêpes, 91
Hangtown Fry, 78, *79*
Hash
Dilled Corned Beef, 67
Turkey Hash with Curry Sauce, 71
Hashed Brown Potatoes, 66
Herring. *See* Kippers
Holland, breakfast foods in, 6
Hollandaise Sauce, 47
Honey Butter, 114
Honey-Pecan Butter, 83
Honey-Wheat Toasting Bread, *110*, 119
Hot chocolate drinks, *17*, 18

I
Irish Coffee, 16
Italian Sausage Bread, *110*, 120
Italian Sausages, Grilled, 64–65

Italian-style breakfasts, 6
Bellini, *22*, 24
Baked Apples with Prunes, *33*, 34
Egg and Vegetable Scramble, 49
Jam-Filled Crescents, *22*, 124, *125*

J, K
Jam-Filled Crescents, *22*, 124, *125*
Joe's Special, *62*, 64
Kedgeree, 74
Kippered haddock (Finnan haddie), 74
Kippers, Broiled, with Sweet-Sour
Onions, 75

L
Lamb Cakes, 68–69
Lamb Crêpes, 87
Leek Quiche, 100–101
Leeks, Poached Eggs with, 48
Lemon, Chunky Sautéed Apples with,
32, *34*
Lemon-Banana Drink, 19
Lemon Drop Teacake, 115
Lemon Sauce, Gingerbread Pancakes
with, 83
Lobster Pie, 77

M
Maple Apple Crisp, 32
Maple-Nut Bran Muffins, *40*, 114
Marsala Cream, Sweetbreads and
Mushrooms in, 64
Meats, 63–65, 67–69, 72. *See also
specific meats*
Melon Balls Spumante, 31
Menus
Breakfast-in-a-Glass, 19
Breakfast in Bed, 97
Eggs Benedict Brunch for Eight, *46*,
47
Fall Family Breakfast, 37
Patio Brunch, 106–7
Swiss Christmas Breakfast, 123
Tailgate Brunch, 72–73
Mexican-style breakfasts
Cheese-Stuffed Baked Green Chiles,
58
Chicken and Chile Crêpes, 86–87
huevos rancheros, 42, *43*
Milk Punch, 24
Mimosa, 23
Mornay Sauce, 48
Moussaka-Style Lamb Crêpes, 87
Muffins
See also English muffins
Apple-Pecan, 113
Cheddar Cheese, *10–11*, 113
Maple-Nut Bran, *40*, 114
Miniature Cinnamon, 112
Orange-Date, *7*, 114
Orange Marmalade, 113
Spiced Cranberry, 113, *125*
Mushroom(s)
Asparagus and Mushroom Crêpes, 90
Joe's Special, *62*, 64
Roulade with Mushroom Filling,
60,*61*
Soufflé with Tarragon, 59
Spinach and Mushroom Omelet,
10–11, 52
Sweetbreads and Mushrooms in
Marsala Cream, 64
Mustard Sauce, Dilled, 72

N
Nectarine-Plum Drink, 19
Nutrition, 6–8, 27
Nutty Baked Apples, 34

O
Omelet pan, 85
Omelet(s), 51–53
basic, 51, 53
Brie and Ham, 52
Curried Vegetable, 53
Shrimp and Avocado, 52
Spinach and Mushroom, *10–11*, 52
Strawberry Blintz, 53
Onions
Baked Artichoke and Onion Frittata,
55
Broiled Kippers with Sweet-Sour
Onions, 75
Orange Batter Bread, *10–11*, 119
Orange Butter, 92
Orange-Date Muffins, *7*, 114
Orange juice, *12*
Mimosa, 23
Tequila Sunrise, *23*, 24
Orange Marmalade Muffins, 113
Oranges, Elegant, 30
Orange Spiced Tea, 18
Oven pancakes, 81, 94–95
Oysters
Crusty Oyster Gratin, 75
Hangtown Fry, 78, *79*

P
Pancakes, 80–92
See also Crêpes
Banana Hotcakes with Honey-Pecan
Butter, 83
Blueberry Yogurt, 82
Gingerbread Pancakes with Lemon
Sauce, 83
Honeyed Oven, 94–95
mixes, 82
oven, 81, 94–95
Quick Buckwheat Blini, 84
specialty pans for, *80*, 85
Spinach Brunch, 84
Swedish, *80*, 83
Toad-in-the-Hole, 94
Parmesan Baked Eggs, *56*, 57
Pastries
See also Cake; Pie(s)
Baked Breakfast Reubens, 105
filled (*en croûte*), 105
filo-wrapped, 104–5
Honey-Nut Crescents (*Rugalach*),
124
Italian Jam-Filled Crescents, *22*, 124,
125
Provençal Tomato Galettes, 108
Ratatouille in a Whole Wheat Shell,
98, 105
Pastry
Almond Press-in, 109
Cornmeal, 103
Crisp Wheat, 50
Egg Pastry for Quiche, 100
Press-in, 109
Rye, 102
Patio Brunch, 106, *107*
Peaches, in Bellini, *22*, 24
Peaches and Blueberries with Cream,
31
Pie crusts. *See* Pastry
Pie(s)
See also Quiche(s)
Fisherman's, 78
Fresh Strawberry Torte, 106, *107*
fruit tarts, 109
Greek Spinach, 104
Piña Colada, *23*, 24
Plum(s)
Fresh Plum Kuchen, 109
Hot Buttered, 30–31

-Nectarine Drink, 19
Popovers, Crisp, 115
Pork and Ham Pâté in Brioche, 108
Pork Sausage. *See* Sausage
Potatoes, 63, 66
Baked Potato Skins, 66
Cottage Fried, 66
Fisherman's Pie, 78
Hashed Brown, 66
Poached Eggs in Baked Potatoes, 48
Poultry. *See* Chicken; Turkey
Prosciutto Baked Eggs, 57
Prunes
Italian Baked Apples with, *33*, 34
Winter Fruit Compote, 32
Punch
Hot Mulled Cranberry, 22
Spirited Milk, 24

Q
Quiche(s), 99, 100–103
Asparagus and Seafood, 101
Blue Cheese, 103
Egg Pastry for, 100
Fresh Salmon, 103
Ham and Cheese Custard Pie, 103
Leek, 100–101
Sweet Corn and Bacon, 106, *107*
Quick breads. *See* Breads, quick

R
Raspberries, in Berries Romanoff, 36
Ratatouille in a Whole Wheat Shell, *98*,
105
Refried Beans, 42
Reubens, Baked Breakfast, 105
Rhubarb, Spiced, 30
Rhubarb Meringue Tart, 109
Rice, Curried, in Kedgeree, 74
Rolls
Baked Nutmeg Doughnuts, 122
Cinnamon-Raisin Buns, 122
Croissants, 121
Italian Jam-Filled Crescents, *22*, 124,
125
Russian Dressing, 105
Rye Buns, 72, *73*
Rye Pastry, 102

S
Salmon
Fisherman's Pie, 78
Fresh Salmon Quiche, 103
Kedgeree, 74
Sangria, 25
Sauce(s)
Blueberry, 96
Custard
Calvados, 60
for Moussaka-Style Crêpes, 87
Dilled Mustard, 72
Hollandaise, 47
Honey Butter, 114
Honey-Pecan Butter, 83
Lemon, 83
Mornay, 48
Nippy Cheese, 67
Orange Butter, 92
Sherried Swiss Cheese, 45
Wine-Cream, 91
Sausage
Breton-Style Sausage and Spinach
Crêpes, 88, *89*
Custardy Baked Sausage Sandwiches,
68
Grilled Italian Sausages with
Peppers, 64–65
Italian Sausage Bread, *110*, 120
Pork, homemade, 67

127

Scallops in Tomato Cream, 75
Scandinavian-style breakfasts, 6
  Heart-Shaped Waffles, 96
  Swedish pancakes, *80*, 83, 85
Scones, Auntie's, 114
Sesame Waffles, 96–97
Shad Roe with Caper Butter, 77
Shellfish. *See* Fish and shellfish
Shrimp
  Asparagus and Seafood Quiche, 101
  and Avocado Omelet, 52
  Breton Seafood Crêpes, 88
  Fisherman's Pie, 78
  Individual Tomato Soufflés with Basil and, 58–59
Sorrel, Poached Eggs with, 44–45
Soufflé(s), 57–61
  Calvados, 60
  Cheese-Stuffed Baked Green Chiles, 58
  Four Cheeses, 57
  Individual Tomato Soufflés with Basil and Shrimp, 58–59
  Mushroom Soufflé with Tarragon, 59
  Roulade with Mushroom Filling, 60, *61*
  Spinach, 58
Spinach
  Breton-Style Sausage and Spinach Crêpes, 88, *89*
  Brunch Pancakes, 84
  Greek Spinach Pie, 104
  Joe's Special, *62*, 64
  Karen's Ham and Spinach Rolls, 67
  and Mushroom Omelet, *10–11*, 52
  Soufflé, 58
Strawberries
  Berries Romanoff, 36
  Breakfast Strawberry Shortcake, 35
  French Toast with, 97
  Fresh Strawberry Torte, 106, *107*
  Strawberry Blintz Omelets, 53
  Strawberry Daiquiri, *23*, 24
  Strawberry Drink, 19
  as vitamin C source, 8, 27
Streusel, Brown Sugar, 115
Swedish Pancakes, *80*, 83
Sweetbreads and Mushrooms in Marsala Cream, 64
Sweet rolls. *See* Rolls
Swiss Baked Eggs, 56
Swiss Christmas Breakfast, 123

T
Tailgate Brunch, 72–73
Tarts, fruit, 109
Tea, 18
Teacakes, Lemon Drop, 115
Tequila Sunrise, *23*, 24
Toad-in-the-Hole, 94
Tomato(es)
  Baked Eggs in Tomato Sauce, 55
  Frittata, 55
  Provençal Tomato Galettes, 108
  Scallops in Tomato Cream, 75
  Soufflés with Basil and Shrimp, 58–59
Tomato juice, 8
  Bloody Mary, 25
Trout, Baked Stuffed, *76*, 77
Turkey
  Hash with Curry Sauce, 71
  Lemony Creamed Turkey in French Rolls, 71
  Monte Cristo Sandwich, 95
  Savory Turkey Crêpes, 91

U, V
Utensils
  blini pan, 85
  coffee makers, 15
  crêpe pan, 85
  frying pans, 8–9
  omelet pan, 85
  pancake pans, *80*, 85
  waffle irons, 85
Vanilla Sugar, 30
Veal and Chicken Filo Rolls, 104–5
Vegetable Frittata, 54
Vegetable Omelets, Curried, 53

W
Waffle irons, 85
Waffles, 81, 96–97
Whole Wheat Crêpes, 87
Whole Wheat Dough, for filled pastry, 105
Whole Wheat Shell, Ratatouille in a, *98*, 105
Wine-Cream Sauce, 91
Wines, 22, 24, 25
Winter Fruit Compote, 32

U.S. MEASURE AND METRIC MEASURE CONVERSION CHART

		Formulas for Exact Measures			Rounded Measures for Quick Reference		
	Symbol	**When you know:**	**Multiply by**	**To find:**			
Mass (Weight)	oz	ounces	28.35	grams	1 oz		= 30 g
	lb	pounds	0.45	kilograms	4 oz		= 115 g
	g	grams	0.035	ounces	8 oz		= 225 g
	kg	kilograms	2.2	pounds	16 oz	= 1 lb	= 450 g
					32 oz	= 2 lb	= 900 g
					36 oz	= 2¼ lb	= 1,000 g (1 kg)
Volume	tsp	teaspoons	5.0	milliliters	¼ tsp	= 1/24 oz	= 1 ml
	tbsp	tablespoons	15.0	milliliters	½ tsp	= 1/12 oz	= 2 ml
	fl oz	fluid ounces	29.57	milliliters	1 tsp	= 1/6 oz	= 5 ml
	c	cups	0.24	liters	1 tbsp	= ½ oz	= 15 ml
	pt	pints	0.47	liters	1 c	= 8 oz	= 250 ml
	qt	quarts	0.95	liters	2 c (1 pt)	= 16 oz	= 500 ml
	gal	gallons	3.785	liters	4 c (1 qt)	= 32 oz	= 1 l.
	ml	milliliters	0.034	fluid ounces	4 qt (1 gal)	= 128 oz	= 3¾ l.
Length	in.	inches	2.54	centimeters	⅜ in.	= 1 cm	
	ft	feet	30.48	centimeters	1 in.	= 2.5 cm	
	yd	yards	0.9144	meters	2 in.	= 5 cm	
	mi	miles	1.609	kilometers	2½ in.	= 6.5 cm	
	km	kilometers	0.621	miles	12 in. (1 ft)	= 30 cm	
	m	meters	1.094	yards	1 yd	= 90 cm	
	cm	centimeters	0.39	inches	100 ft	= 30 m	
					1 mi	= 1.6 km	
Temperature	° F	Fahrenheit	5/9 (after subtracting 32)	Celsius	32° F	= 0° C	
					68 °F	= 20° C	
	° C	Celsius	9/5 (then add 32)	Fahrenheit	212° F	= 100° C	
Area	$in.^2$	square inches	6.452	square centimeters	1 $in.^2$	= 6.5 cm^2	
	ft^2	square feet	929.0	square centimeters	1 ft^2	= 930 cm^2	
	yd^2	square yards	8,361.0	square centimeters	1 yd^2	= 8,360 cm^2	
	a	acres	0.4047	hectares	1 a	= 4,050 m^2	